LOG OF THE CENTURION

Based on the original papers of Captain Philip Saumarez on board HMS Centurion, Lord Anson's flagship during his circumnavigation 1740-44

Leo Heaps

SAPERE
BOOKS

LOG OF THE CENTURION

Published by Sapere Books.

20 Windermere Drive, Leeds, England, LS17 7UZ,
United Kingdom

saperebooks.com

ISBN: 978-1-913518-03-5

For Tamar
who has also returned from a long
and lonely voyage

ACKNOWLEDGEMENTS

There are many thanks owed to many people far more learned than myself, whose life-long pursuit has been the study of historic voyages, such as that undertaken by the crew of the Centurion. Doctor Glyndur Williams' familiarity with much of the material I sought saved me months of aimless wandering in the National Maritime Museum, the British Museum, and perhaps in the Spanish archives of Madrid as well. Roger Knight, PhD solved many problems with his concise mind and factual answers to my countless questions.

The staff of the National Maritime Museum at Greenwich, in particular Sue Rice, were very patient with me. The Earl of Lichfield, a descendant of Anson, offered invaluable suggestions. Students of early voyages of exploration and descendants of the mariners of the expedition volunteered important facts that brought a reality and immediacy to the project. Cecil de Saumarez, GBE was able to recollect with the warmth of family, incidents passed down from one Guernsey descendant to another, to draw the past into the present.

Keiren Phelan worked tirelessly to correlate many aspects of this book and Nicholas Vilag took many photographs, ready to spring into action at a moment's notice and go wherever he was needed.

Altogether, to the many mentioned and unmentioned my thanks are gratefully tendered.

TABLE OF CONTENTS

INTRODUCTION

Anson's 1740-1744 voyage round the world in HMS Centurion was the most famous circumnavigation between that of Sir Francis Drake and those of Captain Cook. Its fame was partly due to the unprecedented amount of treasure captured, amounting to several million pounds in modern money; and partly to the contemporary publication of the vivid narrative of the voyage under the name of the ship's chaplain, Rev. Richard Walter, which became a best seller in many languages. We now know that most of that book was actually written by a professional pamphleteer named Benjamin Robins and that it was supervised by Anson himself. It was therefore something like an official publication, reflecting the views of the commanding officer.

The log by Anson's young first lieutenant, Philip Saumarez, aged twenty-nine, which is printed in the following pages, is thus a welcome addition to the other journals of the voyage because, as a seaman's log, it states the facts without colouring them for publicity purposes. It throws new light on many episodes by providing details not accessible elsewhere. To cite a major example, the climax of the voyage — the capture of the Manila treasure galleon Nuestra Señora de Cobadonga — is not described as the David and Goliath affair which appears in Walter's book but as an extraordinary piece of luck, all the more deserved because of the tenacity of purpose which brought the Centurion to the right spot at the right time. It appears that the Spaniard was actually smaller than the British ship — 700 tons as against 1005 tons burden. Though she carried more men, Saumarez regards it as a piece of madness or criminal negligence on the part of her commander to pit himself against a purpose-built warship of 60 guns. When he led the boarding party over her side Saumarez says he 'was amazed to think what he [the Spanish captain] could propose against our weight of metal and a ship of our appearance.'

The occasion of the voyage was the outbreak of the War of Jenkins' Ear against Spain in 1739. Though the Royal Navy had been sadly neglected during the previous generation, Walpole proposed to make it a maritime war in which the main attack would be made by a fleet under Admiral Vernon on the Spanish colonies in the Caribbean. As a subsidiary operation, Commodore Anson was sent with one third-rate ship and five smaller vessels to raid Spanish commerce in the Pacific (or the South Sea, as it was then called) and to attack towns on the coasts of Chile and Peru. The plan was suggested by two officials of the bankrupt South Sea Company (which never sent a ship to those parts) and another of the East India Company, which wished to see a show of force in the China Seas.

As an operation of war, the strategic inspiration lay much further back in the famous voyage of Sir Francis Drake. He captured the first treasure ship in those seas and had shown how vulnerable were the Spanish possessions in South America. During the seventeenth century his example had been followed by a crowd of buccaneers and privateers, most of whom were too ill-disciplined and too poorly armed to do much harm. However, William Dampier's book about such exploits had been widely read and the one outstanding success (which must have been in the minds of those who planned Anson's voyage) was the circumnavigation by the Duke and Duchess under Woodes Rogers during the previous war. This privateer had captured the Manila galleon on her return to

Acapulco, and he had done just what the Admiralty hoped Anson would do in a King's ship.

The Centurion was certainly better armed than her predecessors, but she was shockingly badly manned. Since Anson was playing a secondary role to Vernon's fleet, his vessels were manned with the utmost difficulty; and since whatever troops which were available were sent to the Caribbean, all that could be provided for Anson's landing parties were 259 old Chelsea Hospital Pensioners, not one of whom survived the rigours of the voyage. The expedition was despatched at the wrong time of year for rounding Cape Horn, its destination was an open secret, and the crews of the ships (numbering 1939 in all) were the worst ever recruited. Of these, 1051 died of disease or exposure, and of the seven ships which left Portsmouth only the Centurion sailed round the world. It is a tribute to her officers that she not only captured the greatest prize at sea, but that she returned at all.

Of these officers six became admirals, and Saumarez would certainly have done so had he not been killed in action later in the war. 'I was born unfortunate,' he told his brother in one of the many depressing moments of this fearful voyage. He lived long enough to purchase a fine house (as Anson did at Shugborough) out of the proceeds of the prize money, but he died before reaching the rank which many of his descendants from the Channel Islands attained in the Royal Navy.

The voyage of the Centurion had little effect on the outcome of the war. It was designed on the outdated pattern of a privateering expedition, the sort of thing which was common in the days of Queen Elizabeth but was ineffective when large fleets of rival nations became the rule. Hence, in the eighteenth century wars with France and Spain fleet actions and fleet blockades became the strategic pattern, not single raiders however heroic. Anson's voyage was the last of its kind.

In terms of human life, it was a disaster. By the time his flagship reached Canton (the first warship to do so) Anson had 201 men left, of whom only 45 were able seamen. The Saumarez log tells the tragic story with its list of deaths day after day: 'April 27, 1741. Our men began to decline apace, the scurvy reigning among us and making terrible havoc.' It is indeed the classic example of the incidence of that scourge of the sea.

Scurvy has always been the curse of long voyages because it is due to lack of vitamin C, the vitamin found in fresh fruit and vegetables, which at that time could not be preserved at sea. Never was a squadron so infamously manned or so badly victualled as Anson's. No one knew what caused the disease, so the only antiscorbutic medicine carried on board was a violent purgative called Dr Ward's Drop and Pill. So terrible were the losses that Dr James Lind, of Haslar Naval Hospital, determined to study the disease. After carrying out the first controlled dietetic experiment on record, he published his *Treatise of the Scurvy* in 1753, which he dedicated to Anson. He could not determine the cause of the disease, vitamins being a twentieth century discovery, but he showed convincingly that the answer was a lemon or an orange — not a lime, which has only half the antiscorbutic content. This discovery was certainly the most important consequence of the voyage, but it took the Admiralty forty years to order the issue of lemon juice after crews had been six weeks on salt provisions. Only by Nelson's day was the conquest of scurvy complete.

The other major disability under which Anson sailed was the ignorance of a method to find out the longitude. Accurate charts of the Cape Horn area were non-existent. Without any means of finding out how far west the ship had sailed, even the master of the flagship underestimated his westing so badly that he turned north too soon. Saumarez was then in command of the little Tryall sloop, which made the same error: 'April 13, 1741. At 1 A.M. discerned land right ahead … probably an island called Cape Noir laying off the Straits of Magellan. This was a most unexpected sight, esteeming ourselves at that time near 200 leagues off.' The same thing happened when the Gloucester tried to rendezvous with the Centurion at the lonely island of Juan Fernandez. It took her four weeks, with her men dying daily of scurvy, to make her landfall, and then she had to be towed to an anchorage because she had not enough men to work the ship.

A cure for scurvy and a chronometer to use in finding longitudes were the two pressing requirements which Anson's voyage demonstrated. Both were to be achieved by Captain Cook on his voyages thirty years later, when for the first time the Pacific Ocean was to be properly mapped. The tragedies, the hardships, as well as the success of Anson's voyage were the precedents of the achievements of his successor in those seas.

Christopher Lloyd

PREFACE

The journals of Philip Saumarez were written daily while he was aboard the Centurion during the voyage to the South Seas and around the world between 1739 and 1744. In effect he kept the fullest logs of the ship. He began the voyage as third lieutenant and ended as captain and second-in-command to Anson.

Some years ago, in Saumarez's ancestral home in the Channel Islands, his four original log books were uncovered in a dirty cardboard box in an old cupboard. With the journals were a wealth of letters and documents that gave an unusual insight into one of the world's great voyages.

Saumarez was a dedicated British naval officer. His careful observations of nature, his descriptions of engagements with the Spaniards, the disease and suffering endured and the capture of the great treasure galleon all display a remarkable character. The journals and letters have put the voyage of the Centurion into a new perspective. The Saumarez journals are the most complete chronicles of the expedition. They form the backbone of this book. However, there is one short exception, the amazing shipwreck of the Wager. This part is culled from the journals of the survivors, Bulkely, Young and Cheap, and other documents listed in the bibliography.

Commodore Anson himself relied upon Saumarez's journals for his famous Letter of Proceedings to the Admiralty, which he wrote from Macao in 1743. Also the popular account of the expedition, issued in 1748 under the name of the Reverend Richard Walter, in large measure uses the details so carefully chronicled by Saumarez.

Philip Saumarez was born in St Peter Port in Guernsey on November 17, 1710. He was a member of a naval family, one of whom fought in the Armada in Elizabethan times under Drake. Thomas, his younger brother, served as midshipman on the Centurion. Philip Saumarez was of delicate health, and service in the Caribbean area early in his naval career further weakened his somewhat fragile constitution. After duty on a number of ships he was finally commissioned to serve aboard the Centurion in 1739 under George Anson. During the voyage of the Centurion he became Anson's first officer and his trusted friend. He was a profoundly sensitive man, highly devoted to duty, his family and friends. He never married: he did not seem to have time. Only in his letters do we find his true, deeply emotional character. When Saumarez led the fleet around the Horn he wrote to Anson from aboard the Tryall. Under stress and depressed from the strain of the unrelenting storms he bared himself in a letter that we are not certain he ever delivered. He laments to Anson that he has been overlooked in promotion and deserves the recompense of a captaincy, while proclaiming his devotion to duty. For a moment the hardships of the voyage had made him drop his guard. Although his later letters and his summary of the voyage written from Macao in 1742 reveal a man of profound sensitivity, he never again permits his emotions to so thoroughly dominate his pen. He was obsessed with the idea of distinguishing himself and strangely prescient of the brevity of his life. Like many of his colleagues he was to the core a professional naval officer and an exceptional human being.

The gruelling hardships of the four year circumnavigation of the Centurion thoroughly exhausted all who survived. When Saumarez had at last recovered a measure of health in the waters of Bath he went on to serve with unusual distinction and commanded his own vessel, the Nottingham, in the war with France. He captured the great French warship the Mars and achieved other notable victories during the short time left to him. In 1747 a cannon ball struck him down as he fought against the French fleet off Finisterre. He was 34 years old. The surgeon who examined his body stated that his lungs were so shrivelled that had he lived he would scarce have had another year of life. In Westminster Abbey there is a monument and a plaque erected to Captain Philip Saumarez, a brave and gifted man. Had he lived there is scarce doubt he was destined to become a great name in naval history.

Admiral Sir John Norris, one of the two protagonists behind the expedition to capture The Acapulco Galleon

CHAPTER ONE: BACKGROUND TO THE VOYAGE

During the first part of the 18th century Spanish administrators in the colonies of the New World were slowly losing control over much of the Indian population upon whose merciless exploitation their well-being depended. Many years of easy living had made the Spaniards soft and complacent and little prepared to defend themselves against a determined enemy. The Spanish Empire was vast. The Caribbean, Central America, lower California, Mexico, Peru, Chile and westward to Manila was all under the flag. Although sugar, tobacco and cotton formed a large part of the mundane wealth of New Spain, in the end it was the greed for silver that drove the English to plunder the Spanish colonies.

France too was aware of the waning strength of her ally in the New World. French sea power was anxious to fill any vacuum left by Spain. French merchantmen from St Malo and Nantes had rounded Cape Horn to trade on the Spanish coast of South America in sizeable numbers and around 1710 they had almost glutted this market with French goods. Meanwhile, British privateers such as William Dampier and George Shelvocke had roamed the South Seas, looting, fighting and exploring. No one knew whether another continent stretched across this endless ocean or whether the South Pacific consisted of nothing more than thousands of small uncharted islands. The Pacific was still unknown, hazardous. Its mysteries had been barely penetrated by Sir Francis Drake, Thomas Cavendish and Richard Hawkins in the 16th century.

In 1669 an indomitable mariner called John Narborough set out from Plymouth in his vessel the Sweep-Stakes. He carried £300 of trade goods and was accompanied by a merchant ship and a Spanish pilot. The Lord High Admiral of England had sent Narborough to establish the foundation for trade with the lucrative markets of Spain. However, the Spanish pilot who accompanied him proved ignorant of the coast of South America. Narborough was left to carry on alone. After passing around the Horn he unsuccessfully negotiated with the Spaniards at Valdivia in Chile where four of his men were imprisoned. He returned home to England through the Straits of Magellan, a disappointed man but the first person to have navigated the Straits both ways.

Narborough charted the waters around Cape Horn with reasonable accuracy and thus made Anson's passage around South America less perilous. He appraised with foresight the true state of Spanish defences on the west coast of America for what they were: a loose association of towns, poorly defended, reaping the uncontested benefits of rich trade with the Indians. But above all he saw that these same towns were exposed to any resolute invader.

English buccaneers since the 16th century had pillaged, burned and fought their way from Valparaiso to Acapulco. Such privateers held letters of marque from the monarch that gave them the authority to wage war against his enemies. But most carried their authority in the defiant note that Captain Sawkins sent to the governor of Panama, when his presence was challenged. He told the governor his crew would 'bring our commissions on the muzzles of our guns at which time he should read them, as plain as the flame of gunpowder would make them.' The governor took the hint and submitted.

Captain Charles Swan in the Cygnet and John Strong in the Welfare in 1690 attempted trade at Valdivia as had Narborough, but they were both repulsed with unequivocal firmness. Spanish trade remained closed to Britain on an official level. Only the buccaneers flourished and grew rich, by taking the law into their own hands.

Some of the buccaneers who preceded the voyage of the Centurion were men of learning with delightful personal qualities. Cut off from their homeland, living off the shores of the Americas, they made their own charts and lived by their wits and strength of character. The lands they touched were largely unknown, 10,000 miles and more away from England. Their 'business was to pillage', as Dampier said. Basil Ringrose explained much of the buccaneers' mentality in his book *Containing the Dangerous Voyage and Bold Assaults of Captain Bartholomew Sharp and Others Performed in the South Seas*. The writings of Lionel Wafer, a 17th century buccaneer-surgeon who travelled to Panama, are still valued by anthropologists for their detailed observations of Indian life.

But perhaps no one among the buccaneers had the same colour and brilliance as William Dampier. He waded through the swamps and rivers of Darien with the journals of his travels rolled up inside a bamboo cane. His stories were classics of travel adventure. His absorbing book *A New Voyage Around the World* was first published in 1697 and those in England who could read devoured it and passed on his story to others so that Dampier became a household hero of his time. Dampier's, Wafer's and Narborough's works, all published before the 18th century, excited a mercantile, powerful England to the prospect of more profitable ventures in the South Seas.

Spain was ailing. The problem over the Spanish Succession created an atmosphere of uncertainty on the Continent while the desire for Spanish wealth became a powerful incentive to successive English governments. Privateers whose efforts at trade had been repulsed by the Spaniards of Chile strongly advocated the establishment of colonies by force. English politicians in the 18th century were slowly coming to the conclusion that time in which to establish their claim by 'force majeure' was running out. Daniel Defoe, the author of *Robinson Crusoe*, was a tireless pamphleteer of the day, a persistent advocate of open trade with Spanish America. He saw the merit of settlement in Chile and indeed even on the River Plate on the Atlantic seaboard. The death of William III in 1702 defeated Defoe's schemes.

The noted geographer Herman Moll in 1711 produced two studied if somewhat incomplete works, charting the known South American coasts within the limit of the all-embracing charter of the new South Sea Company. Moll's limited sources were the printed journals of Narborough, Dampier, Cowley, Sharp and the other privateers who had been there. But all the available information was hopelessly insufficient to make an adequate pilot of this enormous, largely unknown region. One realises from the empty, speculative charts of the day what an infinitely small impression these brave privateers had made on the Great Southern Ocean. By the time the first British naval expedition was ready in 1740 to harass the Spaniards in the Pacific most of the area was still uncharted. Like other navigators of the period, Anson's officers made use of various sources and private accounts, of uncertain accuracy.

By 1739 there was no doubt there would be war with Spain. The war was to be waged on the high seas, far away from home. Despite a less than united administration under Robert

Walpole, harassment of Spanish ships had begun from Cadiz to Havana. The Royal Navy was capable. It was still an outstanding striking force. Its officers were perhaps the finest in the world. But long years of peace had weakened the fleet. There had been no recent great victory to stir the imagination of the nation. A vital manpower shortage starved the navy of crews. The dockyards supplied inferior materials to men-ot-war through corrupt merchants who worked in collusion with equally corrupt officials.

Two major schemes against Spanish-American interests were considered by the government. One was to mount a mighty punitive expedition into the Caribbean under Vice-Admiral Edward Vernon. The other, promoted by Sir Charles Wager, First Lord of the Admiralty, and by Admiral Sir John Norris, was to dispatch four armed naval ships to the Philippines to capture the Manila galleon, the Spanish treasure ship that crossed the Pacific from Mexico. Out of the second scheme the expedition around Cape Horn was born.

It was clear that a triumphant expedition against the Spaniards was needed to raise the political prestige of Walpole's government. This expedition to the South Seas was visualised by Wager and Norris as the last of its kind. It would be conducted in the tradition of the great privateers, yet it would sail under strict Admiralty orders with full naval discipline. It would continue the economic enterprise of the Spanish, Dutch and English voyages to the Pacific, and also be a profitable naval operation against Spain. The treasure ship that sailed between the Philippines and Mexico seemed a delectably rich prize if it could be captured, and this thought remained in the minds of everyone concerned with the venture.

On October 18, 1739 Sir John Norris' intentions were made quite clear to both Sir Charles Wager and James Naish, former influential employee of the East India Company and advisor on the South Sea mission. 'This morning I and Mr Kemp were at Sir Charles Wager's with his secretary Mr Gashry and Mr Naish, who opened to us his sentiments of meeting the Spanish ships from Acapulco at the port of Manila, where they always come to, and likewise are built there and make their outset from thence. And that if a proper strength could be fitted to sail from hence by Christmas we might reach the place before they would arrive with their usual money which is two million sterling or thereabouts. That the Spaniards in the fort and port of Manila were about 150 soldiers; that about 300 soldiers above the ships' complement that should be sent might take the said place, and by removing the Spanish government and garrison, and a good useage to the natives, the place would be easily kept. That by its situation the most beneficial trade can be carried on to China, and if His Majesty should after possession give it to the East India Company an allowable consideration might arise from it. Mr Naish was asked if he would go in the said expedition: to which he said he would be willing and Sir Charles and I were to open it to Sir Robert Walpole alone.'

On November 1 Norris asked who would be the ideal man to command the ships for the Manila expedition. Wager replied that George Anson was the man.

Note: The Acapulco and Manila galleon were different names for the same vessel depending on the port of destination.

A contemporary model of the Centurion

CHAPTER TWO: SHIPS AND MEN

The fleet comprised six fighting ships and two victuallers. The Centurion, the Gloucester and Severn were all fourth rate vessels of the line, the Pearle and Wager were fifth and sixth rate vessels and the Tryall, with eight guns and an overall length of only 84 feet, was the smallest in the squadron, but she was a fine sailer and proved her worth on more than one occasion.

Two merchant victuallers called pinks accompanied the squadron. One of 400 tons burthen was called Anna and the other 200 tons named Industry. Their crew were 14 and 12 respectively. Pink was the name given to a type of vessel with an exceptionally narrow stern.

In the 18th century sailors lived in sub-human conditions. Their quarters below the main deck were unbelievably crowded. Hammocks were slung so close that there was barely room to move. Each man was allowed fourteen inches: the cattle had more space. Ventilation and a little light came from scuttles and hatches which had to be closed in bad weather. Larger vessels had two tiers of gunports; one on the main deck and another one below in the orlop. Usually a third tier broke the line of the quarterdeck and forecastle. On a long voyage the ports were made watertight with oakum and pitch which further decreased ventilation. After a few days at sea the orlop reeked of filth and sweat. Candle light was the only source of illumination and it did little to dispel the constant dark. The officers were quartered more spaciously in the stern and lived several to a cabin with the captain occupying large, furnished accommodation on his own. But the confined quarters in which the men lived, the lack of simple hygiene, filthy clothes and vermin were a fertile ground for the breeding of disease. Anson's squadron's total complement was 1939 officers, men, boys and supernumeraries. In addition to the normal crew the six ships, except the two victuallers, had 552 Marine pensioners and raw recruits divided between them. The already overcrowded quarters this developed a hive like congestion.

Toilets (heads) were built into the bows, over the water. Their exposed position, and the effects of illness, weakness and dysentery meant that quarters below decks tended to stink of sewage at sea on long voyages. Food was eaten by the sailors normally in the limited space between the big guns. If the weather was fine, meals were consumed on deck.

The diet was one of unrelieved monotony. Salted meat came out of the great vats and was served five days a week, and on the banian days, which were Friday and Tuesday, salted fish and cheese were hacked up by the cook and passed to the men from out of the store boxes. Beans, rice, oatmeal and split peas were issued as long as they lasted. Vegetables, consisting of onions and potatoes, soon rotted on long voyages so that the staple diet reverted to either salt pork or salt beef. Meat was pickled in strong brine, and even after steeping increased the thirst. On protracted voyages the water ration was reduced to less than a pint a day per man. Wines, spirits and beer were the usual drinks and large quantities of alcohol were consumed. A sailor was allowed a gallon of beer a day or a pint of wine and a half pint of rum. Biscuit was made of flour and water and had the consistency and appearance of clay, and was broken by either smashing it on deck or splitting it with a hammer. More frequently than not the weevils had already bored through this delicacy before it was issued so that weevil and biscuit were eaten together. Officers kept their own hen coops as well as live geese, goats and cows which were tended below deck, near the men's quarters. The larders of the officers were stocked with private provisions and copious supplies of fine wines. In the year 1739 Majesty's Navy had altered little in its ways since Elizabethan times. The system was cruel, vicious, unrelenting.

It was estimated that half of the sailors in Anson's squadron were the victims of the press gangs who scoured the lanes and houses of English coastal towns looking for crew. Humane men had to turn their heads at barbaric practices. Commodore Anson later showed he could act with humanity once he was away from home. But complete obedience was an officer's lot. There was no deviation from the system, no alternative but dismissal or death. Only through iron discipline was the Navy able to control so many pressed men. Conditions of service were not likely to fill the ranks with happy volunteers. Once a man was at sea there was no way back and he had to make the best of his job, though Anson's voyage held out the distant prospect of Spanish loot which could have been one of the few attractions for the seamen.

There were no more miserable men aboard the ships of Anson's squadron than the Chelsea Pensioners who represented the majority of the Marine Regiment. Indeed, there can be few more repugnant actions in the Royal Navy than the forced recruitment of these ancient veterans of foreign wars who were taken out of retirement from the Chelsea Hospital where they were to spend their last days. Almost all the marines were over sixty years of age, and many were over seventy. A large number were sick or maimed and several had lost their limbs. But a regiment of marines had to be provided by order, and since no other group was available the hospitals of Chelsea were combed until the required number was mustered. Most of these old men were too sick to desert but those who could chose to risk death by desertion rather than face life aboard a naval man-of-war.

The march of the invalids to Portsmouth from Chelsea made a pitiful spectacle. Many of them required medical attention and some had to be carried aboard on stretchers. When Mr Waller, the surgeon for the Centurion, reported that two of the invalids were too ill to go aboard, Anson mercifully sent them to hospital and reported this to the Admiralty. Upon hearing that two pensioners had evaded duty the Lords Justice of the Admiralty immediately ordered them back aboard. Within a month these two old men had died at sea. The Commodore dreaded the fearful death toll of these veterans who, he knew, would never be capable of fighting even if they should stay alive by the time they reached the Great Southern Ocean. A man would need all the strength and vigor of his youth to live out the hardships of this journey. The Lords Justice and the Lords of the Admiralty had cruelly condemned 259 old men to a slow and tortuous death so that they could fulfil a brutal order.

Although the Commodore might have been ashamed of the orders he was forced to obey, he was powerless. Anson had either to obey or be relieved of command.

On October 19, 1739 England formally declared war on Spain. On January 10, 1740 Anson received his orders. In essence he was commanded to round Cape Horn and 'annoy and distress' the Spaniards in the South Seas by 'taking, sinking, burning or destroying all their ships'. Also, he was 'to surprise, or take any of the towns or places belonging to the Spaniards on the Coast'. He was ordered to go as far north as Mexico and California to look for the treasure ship, the Acapulco Galleon. 'You may possibly in that case think it desirable to return home by way of China'. Orders were altered continuously as meetings between Wager, Norris, Walpole and King George II brought forth new priorities and decisions. Everyone considered the Caribbean of first importance. Few of the pompous Lords of the Admiralty could fully understand the meaning of a Pacific venture. It was due more to the prodding of the old East India hands like James Naish than to any foresight of the Admiralty that the Pacific expedition was launched.

The question of how the squadron was expected to harass the Spaniards of America without a proper regiment of foot soldiers has never been answered. One may very well inquire if anyone really cared whether or not Anson succeeded. There were some who suggested that Anson's voyage had been conceived to satisfy a public clamour for action against Spain and no one was really concerned if it failed. The main effort was directed to the Caribbean where a large, well-equipped force was to march on Panama under Lord Cathcart. Everything else was subordinate to this operation. From the outset the expedition to the South Seas was conceived as if it had been designed for disaster.

The ships of Anson's Squadron

Ship: Centurion
Captain: George Anson
Officers and servants: 32
Seamen: 367
Marine Officers: 5
Men: 117
Total ship's company: 521
Overview: 4th rate, 60 guns. 1005 tons, 144 feet in length, 40 feet beam. Built Portsmouth dockyard and launched January 6, 1732. Broken up at Chatham in December 1769. Normal complement: 400.

Ship: Gloucester
Captain: Richard Norris
Officers and servants: 33
Seamen: 254
Marine Officers: 5
Men: 104
Total ship's company: 396
Overview: 4th rate, 50 guns (originally called Gloster). 866 tons, 134 feet long, 38 ½ feet beam. Built at Sheerness dockyard and launched March 22, 1737. Burnt August 16, 1742 near the Ladrones. Normal complement: 300.

Ship: Severn
Captain: Hon. E. Legge
Officers and servants: 36
Seamen: 257
Marine Officers: 4
Men: 87
Total ship's company: 384
Overview: 4th rate, 48 guns. 683 tons, 131 feet length, 34 ½ feet beam. Built by Johnson of Blackwall in 1695. Rebuilt at Plymouth in 1739 at 835 tons, and with 50 guns. On October 19, 1746 she was captured by the French ship Terrible. At the second battle of Finisterre she was recaptured (October 14, 1747) and broken up. Normal complement: 300.

Ship: Pearle
Captain: Matthew Mitchell
Officers and servants: 32
Seamen: 204
Marine Officers: 2
Men: 61

Total ship's company: 299
Overview: 4th rate, 42 guns. 559 tons, 117 feet length, 33 feet beam. Built by Burchett at Rotherhithe and launched August 5, 1708. Rebuilt Deptford in 1726 at 595 tons and sold June 28, 1744. Normal complement: 250.

Ship: Wager
Captain: Dandy Kidd
Officers and servants: 24
Seamen: 81
Marine Officers: 6
Men: 132
Total ship's company: 243
Overview: 6th rate, 24 guns. 559 tons, 123 feet length, 32 feet beam. Purchased November 21, 1739. Wrecked May 14, 1741. Normal complement: 160.

Ship: Tryall
Captain: Hon. G Murray
Officers and servants: 17
Seamen: 50
Marine Officers: 1
Men: 28
Total ship's company: 96
Overview: Sloop, 14 guns. 201 tons, 84 feet length, 23 ½ feet beam. Built by Stacey at Deptford and launched September 6, 1732. Scuttled October 4, 1741. Normal complement: 100.

Ship: Anna
Overview: Pink, victualler. Scuttled August 20, 1741. Normal complement: 16.

Ship: Industry
Overview: Pink, victualler. Normal complement: 12.

CHAPTER THREE: PORTSMOUTH TO MADEIRA

Everyone in England seemed to know about the mission to the Pacific. What was believed to be a well-kept secret soon became common gossip on the streets of every southern coastal town. Foreign intelligence sources brought news to Anson that Spain was also interested in the expedition to the South Seas. The namesake of the great Spanish conquistador Pizarro was to head a group of five ships whose duty was to seek out and destroy the British squadron before it reached Cape Horn.

On December 25, 1739 the Centurion lay quietly at her mooring off Portsmouth Harbour when Philip Saumarez reported for duty. Hundreds of details awaited his attention as the third lieutenant. The quantity of provisions to be taken on board for the circumnavigation was enormous. There would be long periods when the squadron would be ranging along enemy coasts: each ship had to be self reliant.

December 25th 1739.[1] Bearings at noon[2] Portsmouth Harbour
His Majesty's ship the Centurion lately come out of dock, her bottom sheathed and graved laying at her mooring abreast the dock, Portsmouth Harbour. Received my commission from the Commissioner's Office in this port as 3rd Lieutenant of His Majesty's Ship the Centurion. Captain George Anson

---

[1] English dates are all given in the Julian or Old Style, except that the year is taken to begin on January 1, not March 25.
[2] Every day's bearings and position are taken at noon.

Commander. Repaired immediately aboard and found her fitting out with great containing 22,400 pounds, much broken by the driving of the tide. Blew exceedingly hard with severe cold weather. Received 21 pecks of beef — 3463 pieces, 24 jars of oyle — 738 gallons, 5 pints and 10 bags of bread — 1120 pounds. Received 3 pecks, 18 tons. PM. received a ton of water and part of the officers' stores. AM. Received 17 pecks of beef — 2812 pieces, 13 heads of pork — 250 pieces, 15 heads of groats, 107 bushels. Received 24 heads, 14 barrels of flour — 14,692 pounds, 30 bags of bread — 3360 pounds, 6 firkins of butter — 360 pounds, 9 ½ heads of vinegar — 585 gallons. His Majesty's ship the Defiance arrived here from the Downs with a great number of supernumary pressed men. Built up 4 cabins by order of the Navy Board for the marine officers intended on board.

February 24th 1740. Moored at Spithead
Was ordered with 25 men and two midshipmen into a tender called The Happy Greeves to impress seamen for this ship.

March 23rd 1740. Moored at Spithead
In the PM. His Majesty's ships the Namure and Yorke sailed hence for the harbour but the latter running aground was obliged to put back; and I returned with the tender having brought 39 volunteers from Jersey. Three days later in the PM. His Majesty's Ship the Rochester and Chester sailed hence to St Helens with 4 Indiamen and other merchant ships in their convoy.

AM. the second Lieutenant and 27 men sailed hence to impress seamen. At 11 struck yards and top mast.

March 28th 1740. Moored at Spithead
In the PM. received 10 tons of beer, 40 bags of bread, 5 firkins of butter and 12 cheeses. AM. His Majesty's sloop the Drake sailed hence for the river. The carpenters from the yard came on board and cut an air scuttle on each side between the two foremast lower deck ports. His Majesty's ships the Lenox, Rippen, St Albans and Orford sailed hence a cruising. Dried the sails.

From March 28 when the Centurion moved to her new anchorage at Spithead, Saumarez observed hundreds of ships arriving and departing from the Solent, sailing to all parts of the world. East Indiamen and war ships boomed out their thunderous salutes to one another. Occasionally, triumphant British privateers returned escorting prizes captured on the high seas.

April 24th 1740. Moored at Spithead
In the PM. struck yards and top mast. His Majesty's ship the Victory with several merchants arrived here from the Mediterranean and saluted the Admiral. Received a new 6 oared cutter from the yard. His Majesty's ships the Lenox, Kent and Rippen anchored here from cruising in the Bay of Biscay, having brought in with them a Spanish man-of-war of 74 guns and 650 men. This ship was called the Princessa, which the former ships with the Orford took. Received 10 tons of beer and a hog load of wood, with 12 butts and 1 hog of

brandy. His Majesty's ship the Panther and some merchant men sailed hence. AM. our tender with the second lieutenant and 32 men went out to impress seamen in the Channel.

May 9th 1740. Moored at Spithead
Being our guard day fired 5 shot to bring several merchant ships to. PM. the Firebrand fire ship arrived here from the Downs and the PM. the Carolina went into the harbour to clean. Admiral Cavendish hoisted his flag upon the Princess Amelia; the Kent and the Spanish man-of-war went in likewise.

June 12th 1740. Moored at Spithead
His Majesty's ships the Detford and Severn arrived from cruising. Employed in sending ashore our dry provisions to exchange. Received 3 barrels of tar and 1 of pitch.

June 14th 1740. Moored at Spithead
AM. the Tryall sloop arrived here with several transport ships with soldiers from Scotland. His Majesty's ship the Lark anchored here in the harbour and saluted the Admiral — the Swift sloop arrived. Received 20 butts of beer.

June 16th 1740. Moored at Spithead
In the AM. on a survey of mast-makers from the yard on our foremast found a defect of 6 inches over and 12 inches deep about 7 feet below the trestle trees, occasioned by a rotten knot. The mast-makers returned it serviceable by blocking up the hole.

June 19th 1740. Moored at Spithead

PM. His Majesty's ships the Romney, Defiance and Tillbury sailed to the westward with a large convoy of merchant ships, the former bound for Newfoundland and the two latter for Jamaica. AM. His Majesty's ship the Rye arrived here from the river and saluted the Admiral.

June 24th 1740. Moored at Spithead

In the AM. Sir John Norris the Vice Admiral of England rowed through the fleet from the ship with the union flag hoisted in the bow of his boat, attended by all the boats in the fleet, and hoisted the union flag on board the Victory and was saluted by all the ships here with 17 guns each. He returned 21. Received 10 tons of beer. The Commissioners came on board and paid the ship's company 20 months pay to the 30th of last September.

July 19th 1740. Moored at Spithead

Sir John Norris' whole fleet returned and anchored at St Helens, his ship the Victory being disabled by the Lyon running on board her in the night and breaking off her head and rails and at the same time the latter lost her foremast and part of her head. AM. received 20 butts of beer. Received also 6 casks of beef, 4 of pork, 32 pecks of bread, 97 casks of flour and 10 firkins of butter. In the AM. surveyed the first and second cable of the best bower and first of the small, which were all condemned. At noon moved.

August 11th 1740. Moored at St Helens

At 4 PM. Admiral Balchen made the signal to weigh. Repeated the same and got under sail with 12 ships-of-the-line, 8 cruisers and 3 fireships. In all 23 and about 100 transports containing 600 soldiers. My Lord Cathcart commanding the land forces, being on board the Buckingham. At 6 the whole fleet anchored at St Helens per signal, at 7 moored a cable each way in 6 fathoms.

August 24th 1740. The Needles N.N.E. 3 leagues. Peverall point W.N.W.
In the PM weighed and brought up the rear of the transports, the fleet consisting of 127 ships in all.

September 18th 1740. Sailed from St Helens and anchored. The Culver Cliffs N. W. 2 leagues
At 7 AM. made the signal to weigh and made sail with His Majesty's ships the Gloucester, Severn, Pearle, Wager and Tryall sloop, with 2 merchant ships laden with provisions for our squadron. At 10 being calm came to in 10 fathoms.

The squadron was 6 leagues off the Needles. Its orders were to escort as far as the Bay of Biscay convoys bound for the Mediterranean and North America. Then Anson's eight ships would change direction and sail alone for the coast of Brazil.

September 20th 1740. The Ram Head North by West 6 leagues
At 6 PM. the Bill of Portland bore north 4 leagues. Hauled in for Torbay to look for a fleet of merchant ships waiting there for convoy which not seeing away to the Westward. At the Berry Head we hoisted the broad pendant at the maintopmast head, Captain Anson being appointed Commodore of the above mentioned 5 ships.

Received the salute of the squadron which we returned with 15 guns. Came up with His Majesty's ship the Rye and Lively which saluted us. At 11 discerned the Torbay fleet laying to off the Ram Head waiting for us.

September 21st 1740. The Ram Head distance 37 lgs. Lat 49° 06' N. Begin my longitude from London 6° 45' West
The whole part [of the day] moderate and fair. At noon joined His Majesty's ships the Dragon and Chatham with a large convoy of merchant ships bound for America and the Rye bound to Portugal. Severally saluted and at 4 PM. made sail to the Westward with the whole fleet consisting of about 150 ships. AM. several of our convoy being to windward and ahead of us fired several shots to make them bear down to us. At 10 made the Dragon's signal to chase in the southeast quarter after a sloop with French colours which came from Rochelle bound for Cork. Put the ship's company to short allowance of brandy.

Sailing against a great western swell, in large seas and squally weather, the convoy was gradually decreasing in size as the merchant ships bound for Virginia changed direction and departed. Now and then a ship of the squadron would chase an unidentified vessel which usually turned out to be nothing more than a friendly merchantman.

By September 28 the squadron was over 600 miles from Rame Head, shipping heavy seas in bad weather. Fresh gales of wind forced them to reef down constantly as the Gloucester, Severn, Pearle, Wager, Tryall and the two victuallers altered course westward towards the island of Madeira. In the early part of October they met a French man-of-war and a friendly

Dutchman. Otherwise nothing very eventful occurred until the Industry, one of the victuallers, had to be taken in tow. Thus the speed of the entire squadron was slowed and poor progress made for several days until repairs could be completed.

It was already clear that the condition of the ships was such that continual repairs and makeshifts would be necessary, and throughout the voyage this would be the case.

Although the Admiralty had given strict orders to round Cape Horn as quickly as possible, the vessels of the squadron were constantly distracted by necessary diversions against unidentified ships. If Anson wished to hurry to avoid the Spaniards cruising under Admiral Pizarro, his manner certainly did not betray his fears. His attitude and that of his officers was leisurely and calm. They hoped to reach Cape Horn not later than January which was summer in the Southern Hemisphere. But they were unaware that the best time to round the Cape from the east was during the months of June and July. They were sailing for the Horn in the worst possible season when they were likely to meet strong opposing winds of gale force.

After the initial squalls it was a slow journey to Maderia. On some days they made as little as eighteen miles while on others the Centurion would plunge ahead under a fresh breeze with all sail set and log 124 miles or more. After three weeks they were still 300 miles from the island, frustrated by lack of wind and the counter-currents which set them away from their destination. The order was given to put the men on short rations until they reached port.

On October 21 the entire squadron stood to the southward in order to gain the parallel of the island. In the evening the Tryall chased a ship eventually found to be a British merchantman from Liverpool bound for Madeira. The next morning the Gloster, not to be outdone, sighting an unidentified vessel overtook her, but was disappointed to discover she was from Glasgow and heading for the Isle of Man. In the early morning of October 23 a small brigantine from Falmouth joined the Centurion for protection as they approached the coast of Madeira.

By October 25 the squadron had already spent a tedious 40 days at sea. Under the harsh discipline of the petty officers raw recruits were being slowly, if reluctantly, moulded into a trained crew. The boatswains and ships' corporals with their wooden rattans were ready to punish slackness, clumsiness or infringements. The discipline among the marines was probably less severe than normal since their sergeants and officers were mostly too old or sick to be effective.

October 26th 1740. The Ram Head — distance 390 leagues.
Lat N32° 36', Lon 16° 37' W
Sent the Severn and Tryall sloop ahead to discover the island of Madeira. Oughtry and Murry deceased. The next day at 6 AM. saw the island. The southernmost desert bore West by North 4 leagues. In my opinion the situation of the place both in our charts and books is laid down too easterly by a degree or more. It being generally found to be 18° longitude from London but is laid 17° 5' west.

Two days later the squadron was safely anchored in Madeira Roads. The two old pensioners, Amand and Colley, who had been forcibly removed from the Portsmouth hospital by the Admiralty, had died aboard the Gloucester before arriving at the island.

Several weeks of calms in the hot weather had already made the men's quarters below decks unbearable. A number of people were infected with dysentery and fevers by the time harbour was reached. In port, the ships replenished stocks of wood, watered and took on copious stores of Madeira wine for the voyage to Brazil.

An event occurred at Madeira that quickly altered the order of promotion. Captain Norris, because of a lingering illness, was forced to relinquish his command of the Gloucester, and was replaced by Captain Matthew Mitchell. The Tryall which Saumarez was later to command was then taken over by Lieutenant Cheap who had been the first officer of the Centurion. Lieutenant Saunders took Cheap's place and Saumarez was made second lieutenant of the Centurion. Peircy Brett was promoted to third lieutenant. As an artist and draughtsman he was to make a considerable contribution.

Saumarez now wrongly felt that he was overlooked and by right should have been given command. He must have felt at Madeira the same as he did two years later at Macao when he wrote to his brother recalling his command of the Tryall, 'And here I must confess to you I was sanguine enough to flatter myself with some dawn of good fortune, some favourable crisis in my behalf. But I was born to be unfortunate.' This foreboding was constantly in mind through the remainder of his life. In Jamaica in 1737 on the Dunkirk he had been noticeably depressed by the death of so many of his comrades. His first encounter with the cheapness of life aboard a British man-of-war had filled him with a sad fatalism from which he never recovered. One senses that Saumarez's destiny had been decided at the age of thirty when he met Anson; that his character and philosophy of life had been set.

The governor of Madeira reported that seven Spanish war ships had been cruising to the westward of the island during the previous week. There was little doubt that this was the squadron led by Admiral Pizarro. Anson despatched a small boat out beyond the island for reconnaissance but the Spanish men-of-war could not be seen. It was surmised, correctly as was later discovered, that the Spaniards still thought the English squadron was in company with Admiral Balchen's large fleet with whom they had left St Helens. This miscalculation was the first of many Pizarro made in chasing an enemy whom he saw only briefly and who eventually led him to disaster. Whenever he was faced with a decision Pizarro seemed always to make the wrong choice. When he finally guessed correctly that the English were really on their way to Cape Horn he rushed out from his refuge on the River Plate without adequate food or water, and wrecked all his ships but one along the rugged shores of Patagonia.

CHAPTER FOUR: CROSSING TO SOUTH AMERICA

On November 3, 1740 the squadron weighed anchor from Madeira Roads. Anson had issued written instructions that the next rendezvous was St Julians, but once at sea he reconsidered. St Julians in Patagonia was too distant and the season was already too far advanced. Instead, the squadron would sail the 1800 miles of open ocean to the equator and then another 1300 miles to the island of St Catherines on the coast of Brazil. This would be their last stop but one, before they were to set out around the Horn. Instead of the steady northeast trades they had expected the winds blew from the wrong directions, impeding their progress. By the end of the first week at sea, however, the winds shifted to the right quarter and they began to make good speed.

November 14th 1740. The Island of Madeira — distance 781 leagues. Lat N15° 46', Lon 28° 03' W
Continuance of fair weather. Altered our course for a supposed shoale called the Palmas bearing about S.S.W. 80 leagues distance from Antonis. Found the variation by amplitude to be 03° 35' W.

November 17th 1740. The Island of Madeira distance 466 leagues. Lat N10° 40', Lon 26° 37' W
In the AM. brought to and made the signal for all Lieutenants to give them orders to send the longboats to unburden the Industry laden with brandy, and accordingly began working on her.

November 20th 1740. The Island of Madeira distance 716 leagues. Lat N07° 59', Lon 26° 45' W

At noon completed unloading the brandy vessel each ship having taken his proportion. Ours amounting to 42 casks, having supplied her with several empty casks to fill with salt water for ballast. At 6 P.M. parted with her who steered away for Barbados. Variation by amplitude 01° 14' W.

The officers took amplitudes at regular intervals. An amplitude was a bearing taken on a celestial body such as the sun at sunset. This permitted the navigator to correct the variation in the compass. The compass was subject to continual correction. Measurement by log of the distance run along the compass course, the noon latitude sight, and soundings were the only means of determining position.

When the Industry had signalled the Commodore and came alongside the Centurion, the master explained he had come the required distance fulfilling the terms of his charter and now wished to be dismissed. The cargo, as Saumarez reported, consisting mainly of brandy, was distributed among the already overloaded ships of the squadron. However, the master was also given mail from the squadron's crews and dispatches from Anson to the Admiralty. Unfortunately, none of the letters ever arrived. Before she reached Barbados, the victualler was captured by a Spanish warship and the entire crew remained prisoners for three years.

The weight of the newly acquired stores from the Industry pushed the vessels of the squadron deeper into the water, with the effect of having to close most of the ports against the seas at a time when the crews were suffering from the excessive heat of the Doldrums. 'Fever and fluxes' began to attack the men, especially the Chelsea Pensioners. No one could explain the cause, but illness became widespread. The Commodore ordered without delay that scuttles should be cut in all the ships wherever possible for ventilation. This helped a little, but did nothing to alleviate the terrible overcrowding. Mr Waller, Anson's private surgeon, became sick and died suddenly. Although the cause was unknown, it was considered to have been heat and exposure. It also might have been typhoid or dysentery. Near the Equator they drifted in long periods of torpid calm while a scorching sun seared the decks. Below decks, in spite of the new scuttles the Centurion was like a stinking cauldron.

November 24th 1740. The Island of Madeira distance 787 leagues. Lat 04° 31' N, Lon 27° 25' W
This day was more settled than the others but with frequent intervals of squalls and showers. Several of our men through the moisture and inconstancy of the air were attacked with fever and headaches. Not having had an observation through these last days found by this day's observation that I was 15 miles to the northward of my reckoning which confirms the general opinion of a northwest current setting near the equinoctial line.

November 25th 1740. The Island of Madeira distance 611 leagues. Lat 03° 27' N, Lon 28° 09' W
Today had a serene cool air with a constant wind at south east. We now flatter ourselves to be got into a Trade Wind. By an azimuth found ourselves with no variation.

November 26th 1740. The Island of Madeira distance 635 leagues. Lat 02° 25' N, Lon 28° 09' W

The whole part a constant moderate gale with fair weather. Our people still continuing sickly. Richard Pearce an invalid deceased.

November 27th 1740. The Island of Madeira distance 669 leagues. Lat 00° 52' N, Lon 29° 47' W

Found the variation by amplitude to be 16' E. This morning saw several birds which we conjectured came off the island of St Pauls, that place bearing by account north 18° 16' E. Distance 90 leagues. This night looked out for a place called Abrohles lagoon shown by some charts near here. For 48 hours blew a gale.

November 28th 1740. The Island of Madeira distance 708 leagues. Lat 00° 59' S, Lon 30° 20' W

At 1 PM. imagined we passed the equinoctial line in 30° west from the meridian of London. Accounting found the variation to be 11° 36' easterly. At noon the island of Ferdinando Loronso bore 53° 10' W. Distance 90 leagues. Our sick people begin to recover daily chiefly owing to the coolness and temperature of the air.

November 29th 1740. Island of Madeira distance 746 leagues. Lat 02° 45' S, Lon 30° 46' W

It blew a constant fresh gale. A severe clear sky. Pursuing our course to the south west. Amos Gordon and Edward Major, seamen, departed this life.

The surgeons and their mates treated the sick with the 'drops', a purgative that was supposed to cleanse the system but more frequently made the victim deathly ill. The pensioners as usual suffered most. Some managed to crawl to the exposed heads in the bow to relieve themselves after having been treated with drops. But most of them simply remained where they were, lying half-dead in their hammocks with no relief from the diet of salt beef, pork and the indigestible biscuit. Since leaving Madeira there had been 90 deaths. Although many men were sick and dying, as long as there were enough people to work the ship, life carried on as usual.

December 10th 1740. Island of Madeira distance 1121 leagues. Lat 20° S, Lon 38° 34' W

Moderate and hazy with showers and rain. The Tryall sloop being sent ahead to sound made a signal at having ground on which we brought to and sounded in 60 fathoms. Coarse ground with broken shells. We attempted it at 8 AM. with 150 fathoms but had no ground. The Tryall had 37 fathoms then 38 fathoms and then lost the bank. Likewise by this we may conjecture it is steep-to and probably may be very dangerous. It being night prevented making any further discovery, but some books report it to have rocks right up to the water's edge. It is called the Abrohlos. I then esteemed myself in the latitude of 19° 25' S and 60 leagues due East from the coast of Brazil, but others on board were 80 to 80 leagues off. At 4 made sail having altered our course from the South West to South by West. Found our variation to be 06° 51' E.

December 12th 1740. Island of Madeira distance 1186 leagues. Lat 23° 10' S, Lon 39° 32' W

At 6 PM. saw a sail standing to the southward which we chased and at 7 spoke with her being a Portuguese brigantine from Rio de Janeiro to Jodus Sanchos. Next day the Tryall sloop was ordered to go ahead to sound in the night. At 9 AM. Mr Robert Weldon our purser being quite worn out departed this life. Variation by amplitude 09° 30' E.

December 14th 1740. Island of Madeira distance 1286. Lat 26° 48'S, Lon 44° 01' W
Very uncertain squally weather with rain. Esteemed the island of St Katharina to bear South 80° 1' W distance 80 leagues. David Redman a marine departed this life.

December 16th 1740. Island of Madeira distance 1298 leagues. Lat 26° 27' S, Lon 46° 37' W
Generally moderate and cloudy with some few squalls of rain. Sounded frequently but found no ground. Esteemed the Island of St Katharina S57° W distance 39 leagues.

December 17th 1740. Island of Madeira distance 1776. Lat 27° 30' S, Lon 48° 53' W
Found a strong current setting to the southward having carried us 43 minutes to the southward of our reckoning. Fresh gales, the latter moderate. At 4 AM. the Tryall sloop struck ground in 100 fathoms and fired a gun. At 7 discerned the land high and mountainous off the coast of Brazil from the West to West South West about 17 leagues off. At noon a low land which we took to be St Katharina bore West South West 10 leagues, scarce discernable for the high land.

On December 18 the island of St Catherines was finally sighted

as well as the island of Arvoredo. A cluster of small islands
deceptively hid most of St Catherines as the Centurion slowly
and cautiously made her way over the soft, muddy seabed,
sounding continuously with the lead. By 11 pm on the same
day the Centurion steered in under drastically reduced sail for
the northern part of the island where there appeared to be
plenty of deep water.

Admiral Anson

December 19th 1740. Sailing between the Island of St Catherines and the continent of Brazil

At 4 North North West 4 leagues off the Island, made the signal to anchor having sailed in between the island Arvoredo and the north end of St Katharina meeting with regular soundings decreasing from 25 to 12 fathoms. The best bower was laying to the South East. We experienced here a regular tide setting North North West at 2 miles an hour. Tide flood coming from Southward. We discovered 2 fortifications not quite completed, one laying on the western side of St Katharina and the other a small island near the continent of Brazil about 10 miles off. On discovering of us they hoisted the Portuguese colours and fired several guns to alarm the island. To prevent their discomfort the Commodore sent the boat with an officer to acquaint the governor of his arrival, and desire of a pilot. The next morning we weighed and sailed with the squadron between the island and the continent, which forms a very commodious harbour. A pilot from the governor meeting us. Our soundings we observed to decrease gradually as we ran up but found the water deepest on the Continent side there being a large flat laying from the island. At noon were abreast a small island on the St Katharina's side called Parrot Island, a little below a small fortification laying on the point of the above mentioned island.

December 20th 1740. Sailing south, squadron abreast Governor's Island in St Katharina's Harbour

The weather extremely hot and sultry but cool and refreshing at night. Anchored with the squadron on the

Continent side in a large commodious bay called by the French Bon Port, in 6 fathoms about 8 or 9 miles from the place we weighed from. At 8 moored in 5 ½ fathoms. Put out the best bower to the East South East. The ship was about 2 miles from the shore. The ensuing part of the day was employed in sending the boats on both shores to discover the most commodious watering places. Preferred the island side as being most convenient for raising of tents the other side being steep-to and covered with impenetrable woods.

December 21st 1740. Moored in St Katharina's Harbour
Half past noon we passed by the island the governor resides on, saluted the fortification with 11 guns. The same number was returned. Immediately at I made the signal to anchor in 5 ½ fathoms having run as near the island as the shoals and reefs of the water would permit us. Soon after moored with the best bower near St Juans' castle on the island side near the governor's island. The island of St Antonio laying in the middle of the harbour to the south. This evening unbent our sails and in the morning sent all our empty casks ashore on St Katharina's Island where the squadron was to build tents. The harbour formed by the island and the continent is in all respects conveniently adapted for the reception of ships — equally with regard to the security of laying there as to the refreshments it abounds with. The entrance is about 5 miles in breadth laying from thence to the island of St Antonio in the middle of the harbour and near which we anchored. Two isthmuses form a narrow strait one quarter of a mile broad only navigable by boats and small vessels scarce having about

2 fathoms and half water in it — to prevent which they were expecting to erect a battery on the island side which will effectually stop the entrance of an enemy at that end; but unless it were a particular scheme of surprising the ships no fortification can obstruct the entrance of a squadron especially when a sea breeze is made which blows directly and generally very fresh. There is a regular fortification laying on the north and likewise on the south side, but none of them seem calculated for resisting ships of war and probably are more designed to prevent privateers from annoying them and to preserve an appearance among the native Indians with whom they are generally at war. The French who were first having recommended this place generally anchor in a deep bay on the Continent side which they give the name of Bon Port, laying 3 miles to the north of the governor's island where you may ride in 6 or 7 fathoms of water which is more commodious for watering if you design not to make any stay there. The ground everywhere is excellent. Ships need not fear driving if their anchors and cables are good. The southerly winds blow strongest and raise a short hollow sea very suddenly which is as soon over when the gale is ceased. The water both on the island and the Continent is excellent and preserved beyond what I ever observed. After having it on board some short time it discharged itself with a green putrid scum which subsided to the bottom and left the remainder as clear as crystal. We watered on the island sides, it running in a small stream down the rocks which we conveyed in spouts to the casks. About two miles to the northward of the watering place on St Katharina's side, is the Small Plantation and

house, standing on an eminence and situated opposite the governor's island. Nearby there is a large creek which runs a mile and a half inland of the northward of which opening we erected tents for the sick on a tolerable large spot of level ground which was clear of woods, and for that reason recommends itself as affording room for exercise; but its situation was low and liable to be overflown whenever it rained hard which happened more than once. The above mentioned straits divide the harbour into two parts but the southern one is incapable of holding ships the water being too shallow. At the southern entrance of the straits is a small town on the island side called La Villa de St Katharina consisting of nearly 40 houses which is as yet in its infancy being lately begun. The Bay of Arazatibu on the Continent side has likewise a village laying off to the south side of the island where there is anchoring in 5 or 6 fathoms of water, which would be convenient for purchasing of cattle which are very plentiful thereabouts, were it not for the ships being so much exposed to the winds which blow at times very hard and occasion a great sea and few frequent it. Notwithstanding what hath been advanced in favour of this place there is one objection which will always be of weight with those who are embarked in any armament against the Spaniards; which is the vicinity of this place to the River Plate to which they never fail to give information of any expedition designed against them. The air here is likewise extremely hot and sultry from the reflection of the hills on each side of you which are exceptionally high and prevent free interchange of circulation. Till 8 or 9 in the morning a thick fog almost obscures the land and continues until either the sun gathers strength and dissipates those vapours or a brisk sea breeze disperses them. This renders the air close and humid and occasions many fevers and fluxes among us. Another inconvenience which we did not altogether experience but yet we are not quite exempt from, the scheme not being perfected, is an innovation in the governor of this place which hitherto has been the rendezvous of fugitives and outlaws who just acknowledge the subjection to the Crown of Portugal, but in all other respects are quite licentious and have only an obscure person residing amongst them as their captain, commonly sent by the governor at Lagons, a small place to the southward of this island. At present they are modelling it after the same plan that the rest of the principal ports on the coasts are governed by, having for their governors when we were there, a general officer who is likewise an engineer and kept them under severe injunctions. This alteration proceeds from a discovering they have lately made of some valuable gold mines and quarries of diamonds on the Continent side which had encouraged them to send colonists from all parts to settle it. This was the reason which they alleged when we complained of their concealing refreshments from us, that they reserved them for the 100 families whom they daily expected. This joined to the natural circumspection of these people who are jealous of all foreigners coming in their ports and contribute what they can to render it disagreeable, will in short time render the port perfectly inhospitable.

The island of St Catherines was measured by Saumarez to be

30 miles long and its latitude and longitude were correctly recorded. Having thus calculated its exact position Saumarez proceeded to correct his charts. Although the island was quite large, its discovery by ship demanded exacting navigation. The coast of Brazil tended to obscure St Catherines, the mountains of the mainland being high and blending into a number of small surrounding islands. A strange ship coming in from the sea had to approach with caution.

> When coming near it is chiefly distinguishable by an assemblance of small islands lying at each end and scattered along the eastern side of it. The entrance to the harbour is on the north end where if ships coming from the sea sail in between the island Alvorado and the island Galleo and the north end of the island they enter without the least apprehension or danger, being guarded by their lead.

The Saumarez manor on Guernsey, bought with part of the prize money awarded to Philip Saumarez

Saumarez's observations of the land and its people were

accurate and detailed. He spent long hours and many days exploring the island and his knowledge appeared comprehensive. At the time not much was known about St Catherines by the outside world and Saumarez's observations must have been one of the most complete chronicles of the day.

The soil on this island is truly luxuriant and every way flatters the indolence of the inhabitants. There are fruits of most sorts with many vegetables growing spontaneously. It is one continuous chain of trees which enjoy a perpetual verdure but are impenetrable besides a few secret paths the inhabitants have made and a few spots cleared for their plantations which are dispersed along the shore facing the Continent. The natives are chiefly Portuguese with a promiscuous mixture mingling with fugitive Europeans, blacks and Indians. All subject to the Crown of Portugal, all provided with arms, the former quite lawless but now the face of things is changing amongst them as I have observed. Elsewhere there is great plenty of fish of various kinds, all excellent. The woods abound with several medicinal and aromatic plants. One might imagine oneself in a druggist's shop. As you traverse the woods the fruits are chiefly the orange, lemon, lime, citron, melons, grapes, guavas, with pineapple and many potatoes and onions. Here is great plenty of oxen with many pheasants, inferior to ours, but with abundance and monkeys and parrots all edible. They have a very singular bird called the toucan whose plumage is red and yellow with a long beak resembling a tortoise shell and somewhat in the shape of a feather in lieu of a tongue.

St Catherines was a haven for smugglers. Silver and gold were briskly traded with the visiting Spaniards. Inland from the coast were large, valuable diamonds that could be mined on the surface of the hills. The Indians still fished with hooks hammered out of gold-bearing ores while the officials and many of the natives dined with everyday utensils made of precious metals. Not the least active of Portuguese smugglers was the governor himself, Jose Sylva de Paz. In order to ingratiate himself with his Spanish accomplices he had sent a special messenger to Pizarro, who was anchored with his squadron at Maldonado about 600 miles away at the mouth of the River Plate. However, the unexpected delay in repairing the masts of the Tryall caused Pizarro to miscalculate. Upon receiving the news of the English squadron he immediately set off to intercept it. Fortunately, Anson had not left St Catherines. When Pizarro discovered his error the English had already sailed south while Pizarro sailed north, neither seeing the other.

St Catherines was one of the few semi-civilised settlements on the east coast of South America. But it was still a lawless refuge of bandits and privateers. An unarmed stranger was unsafe from the settlers who mistrusted all foreigners, or from the Indians who hated their masters. Gold, silver and diamonds were the currency which was obtained from the natives, who willingly exchanged these valuables for finished European goods. The crew of the English squadron having little to use as barter had traded the clothes off their backs for silver and gold trinkets. In the freezing cold of Patagonia they later regretted their rashness.

In the hospital tents little change could be noticed in the condition of the sick. Very few seemed to improve. The dysentery and fevers did not lessen and the climate, instead of healing the men, actually had an adverse effect. The fresh fruit was a delicious feast for those who could enjoy it. But as the days passed more were stricken with fevers and many who finally sailed worsened and died. No one knew the exact cause of the fever, but the sick were deluged with 'muscatos' and stung at night by millions of gnats. No doubt these insects were disease carriers. Over a hundred years later Darwin on the Beagle reports having come down in Brazil with a debilitating fever which was due to the bite of a poisonous sand fly.

Every morning the ground was damp and covered with fog. Frequent cloud bursts flooded the tents. The surgeons were at a loss to know how to treat the diseases that rampaged through the squadron. The number of sick rose from 300 to almost 350 and of the 78 or more men who died on the island 28 were from the crew of the Centurion. Most of the casualties were among the old Chelsea Pensioners who had no resistance left to fight off illness.

On December 27 a strange sail was sighted far out to sea. A crew of 18 were sent by the Commodore in the cutter to intercept. The vessel turned out be a Portuguese brigantine, which was treated courteously by the English who apologised for their mistake. However, the governor of St Catherines made a great display of being insulted by the crews' behaviour, which led the Commodore to suspect that the squadron had now outlived its welcome on the island. At the earliest possible opportunity he decided to take his leave. It would be none too soon for the crew. Even the sick would be glad to leave this inhospitable place.

When repairs to the rotten mast of the Tryall were finally completed, fresh provisions were taken on board the ships. Dozens of oxen were slaughtered, the ships' bins piled high with new-picked fruits, onions and potatoes, and the sick tents were dismantled. The decision was made to weigh anchor with the tide. On January 18, 1741 the squadron left the wide harbour of St Catherines and set sail southward to Port St Julian in gloomy weather. Henceforth, all the Pacific coast of South America was Spanish.

CHAPTER FIVE: ARRIVAL AT PATAGONIA

A signal was made once out of sight of St Catherines, for the captains to come aboard the Centurion to receive their orders. If Anson was incapacitated and unable to give commands the expedition was to carry on and fulfil its mission with all the remaining men, vessels and strength at its disposal. The next rendezvous, at Port St Julian, was 1200 miles south on the desolate coast of Patagonia. From there a further 500 miles stretched between the squadron and the Straits of Le Maire, at the east tip of Cape Horn. Once round the Horn they would carry out their mission in the Southern Ocean. After the conference the officers returned to their ships.

Later a thick fog suddenly enveloped the squadron followed by an easterly storm of considerable violence with winds gusting to over 60 knots, which swept down upon them, driving the ships towards a lee shore and separating the formation. The weather was unchanged for three days and on the fourth day when it cleared, Saumarez, surveying the sea for a sign of other members of the squadron, reported that only the Tryall was visible. She was far off to leeward, and carrying sail on only one mast. The main mast was broken about four feet short of the top. All the yards had completely vanished. She was sailing at much reduced speed and labouring heavily in the large swell left by the storm.

One by one all the boats reappeared later in the day, except the Pearle. She was nowhere to be seen. In the meantime the Gloucester, the second largest man-of-war, took the Tryall in tow.

February 14th 1741. The Island of St Katharina 500 leagues. Lat 47° 43' S, Lon 69° 35' W

These 24 hours moderate and hazy weather as we run along shore with our squadron. Take this Cape to lay in 69° 30' W. At 4 P.M. saw Cape Blanco bearing South West. It is chiefly distinguishable by it being a large round homock with some white cliffs facing it, and particularly by a small island called Penguin Island, a flat, low rocky place generally covered by those birds whence it is called. We fell suddenly from 36 fathoms to 24, 19 and 14 fathoms on which we hauled from South East to the North West. Soon after it deepened again to 15, 17, 26 and 32 fathoms of gravelly ground. We then altered our course and coasted again along shore. The land here seemed to trend away to the South West. The variation was 20° E.

A south-going current running strongly down the Brazilian coast helped the expedition make good time towards their rendezvous at St Julians. As the squadron approached the Cape the weather turned decidedly colder. In the evening there were occasional snow flurries and in the morning the decks were covered with frost. The seas were larger too; long, deep swells, with breaking crests, surrounded them. There was also a sterile barrenness to the landscape. Enormous rocks and cliffs and shapeless crags hung like huge claws above the sea. The list of men dead from disease mounted slowly and steadily as they sailed south in sight of Patagonia. Few of those who had ailed at St Catherines recovered.

February 16th 1741. The Island of St Katherina — 431 leagues. Lat 48° 54' S, Lon 70° 04' W.

Unchanged weather. Coasting along shore in regular soundings from 53 fathoms to 45 fathoms. At 6 PM. tried the current and found it setting South South West. At 6 PM. the land bore from the South West to the North West 9 leagues. At noon saw the land. A low flat even land all along.

February 17th 1741. The Island of St Katherina — 434 leagues. Lat 48° 54' S, Lon 70° 37' W

There was little winds and thick foggy weather, and kept coasting along shore in quest of St Julians' Harbour and found regular soundings as we approached the shore — from 40 fathoms decreasing gradually to 25. Black sand. At 5 PM. made the signal for the squadron to anchor and came to with the best bower in 26 fathoms. A flat low rock laying about 2 miles off shore bearing North West by North 5 miles. At 4 AM. made the signal to weigh and plyed to the southward. At 6 AM. saw a sail to the southward of us which we judged to be the Pearle and therefore made the signal for all cruisers, but she standing off sent the Gloucester to chase. At 9 the weather proving squally with rain and took in the topsail.

On February 18, almost one month after the squadron had lost contact with the Pearle, a vessel was sighted on the horizon. Although everyone suspected it might be the Pearle no one was absolutely certain. The Commodore, in doubt, gave immediate order to chase. The Pearle at first nervously set more sail as if making ready to flee from a possible enemy, but upon recognising the Gloucester she turned round and joined her. She then sailed up to the Centurion's stern to report on her long absence. The news was sad. Captain Dandy Kidd was dead. He had died two weeks before from a nameless fever that had made him delirious for many days, and mad during his last hours. Lieutenant Salt, who at his captain's death assumed command of the Pearle, explained the reason for his somewhat timid behaviour at sighting the squadron. He had made a near-fatal mistake some days ago which he did not want to repeat. He had almost joined the company of five Spanish men-of-war under Pizarro thinking they were members of his own squadron. After one of the Spanish ships had raised English colours as a ruse, Salt noticed that their pennant was flying the wrong way from the masthead. He discovered the error just in time and escaped by boldly sailing over a patch of rippling current which the Spaniards, believing it to be a shoal, avoided. Salt, guessing correctly, glided with his shallower draft through the broken waters to safety while his enemy turned back.

From February 19 to February 25, 1741, the squadron anchored outside Port St Julian, not wishing to risk crossing over the sandbar at the entrance which could put the ships aground at low water. Tactically, it was too dangerous to go right into the harbour with the possibility of Pizarro's fleet nearby, although it certainly would have been more comfortable. Repairs had to be made to the broken mast of the Tryall with the inadequate materials at hand. She was jury-rigged with reduced sail set from the stump of the broken mast. Later, when the expedition was struck by the ferocious gales off the Horn, this reduced sail was to save the ship from foundering as she led the squadron through the constant storms. Although there were several hundred men still very sick there is no record of further burials at St Julians.

In 1670 Narborough had reported that 'there was not enough wood in Patagonia to make a handle for an ax'. And he was right; the landscape had not changed in seventy years: not a single tree could be seen. But abundant grass inland made it a refuge for thousands of wild cattle that had multiplied from the few left behind many years before by some farsighted Spaniards, providing fresh meat for Anson's squadron when it called at this lonely harbour during the winter of 1741.

St Julians was a dark and foreboding place with a morbid history. Magellan in 1520, when he discovered the harbour, had quelled a mutiny there. He hanged the mutinous leader at a place he named Gallows Point; and not far away killed another and marooned two more of his crew on the shore. In 1578, when Francis Drake took refuge at St Julians, he found the remains of the gallows left by Magellan. Drake had held a court martial in the harbour on a small island which he called the Island of True Justice. It was here that Drake's companion, Captain Thomas Doughty, for mutinous behaviour and 'producing contrary winds by black magic' was condemned to death. He died after having joked with Drake over a drink. Both men had been close friends. The grotesque frippery of the execution was typical of the Elizabethan era. Death and tragedy hung over this grim place.

The death of Captain Dandy Kidd, a relative of the famous buccaneer, had as Saumarez said, 'caused a revolution in promotion among us'. Anson's former first lieutenant on the Centurion, David Cheap, was elevated to captain of the doomed Wager. Cheap was to play an important role in the sad future of that vessel and the events that arose out of shipwreck. Meanwhile, Saumarez was moved up to the rank of first lieutenant of the Centurion, directly under Commodore Anson. Fortune was to give him opportunity to prove himself earlier than he expected. Lieutenant Saunders, the Centurion's first lieutenant, was advanced to command the Tryall, but suddenly became seriously ill. Since it was impossible to move Saunders from his cabin on the Centurion without grave risk to his health, Saumarez temporarily took over command of the Tryall. For seven weeks he was to lead the squadron around the Horn through some of the worst weather of the entire voyage.

By Commodore George Anson Esq
Commander in Chief of his Majesty's ships
designed on a particular expedition

Whereas Captain Charles Saunders his Majesties Sloop Tryall, is taken ill of a fever on board the Centurion, and as 'tis the opinion of the Surgeons in the Squadron that removing him on board his Sloop, in his present condition may tend to the hazard of his life.

You are therefore hereby required and directed to repair on board his Majesties said Sloop Tryall, and act as Master and Commander in her during Captain Saunders present ill state of health, strictly charging and commanding all the officers and Company of the said sloop in their several Employments to behave themselves jointly and severally with all due respect and obedience to you their said acting Master and Commander and you are duly to execute all such orders and Commands as you shall from time to time receive from me or any other your Superior Officers for his Majesties Service during your continuance on board her, hereof you nor any of you may fail, as you will answer the Contrary at your Peril and for so doing this shall be your Order Given under my hand on board his Majesties Ship Centurion at St Julians this Twenty fourth day of February 1741.

To Mr Philip Saumarez first Lieut,
of his Majesties Ship Centurion and
appointed Acting Master and Commander
of His Majesties Sloop Tryall

G. Anson

When the repairs had been completed on the Tryall two places of future rendezvous were carefully selected. The first was the island of Nuestra Señora de Socorro, now known as the island of Huamblin. This was 300 miles south of Valdivia off the Chilean coast. The alternative rendezvous was Juan Fernandez, an island 370 miles due west of Valparaiso in the Pacific Ocean. With long passages ahead the decks of the ships were stripped of excess cargo, which was transferred to the Anna. Guns which had been lashed below at St Catherines were brought on deck and the heavy gun carriages were remounted ready for action. Anson believed that there was immediate danger of battle with the elusive and now hopelessly lost Spanish squadron which searched for the British off Patagonia. Regardless of the weather, he must be ready to fight the Spaniards at any time.

On February 27 the squadron weighed anchor.

February 27th 1741. Woods Hill distance 4-5 leagues
The 24 hours moderate and cloudy. Lieutenant Saunders being extremely ill at the time of his being appointed Captain of the sloop and incapable of being removed on board her, I received an order from the Commodore to take on me the command of the sloop during his illness and accordingly I repaired on board. At 6 AM. the Commodore made the signal to weigh. At 10 I purchased my anchor and got under sail being ordered ahead of the squadron. At noon it beginning to blow fresh took in 1 reef in the topsails.

February 28th 1741. Woods Hill distance 12 leagues
The first part fresh gales and hazy with rain, the middle and latter proved moderate and fair. At ½ past noon the whole squadron was underway excepting the

Gloucester, who we left purchasing her anchor. At 1 PM. wore per signal and stood to the northward in wait for her. At 12 PM. tacked per signal and stood to the South East quarter. At 6 AM. were joined again by the Gloucester who had left her anchor behind. At 8 had regular soundings from 38 to 40 fathoms of soft ground.

March 1st 1741. Woods Hill at St Julians distance — 17 leagues. Lat 49° 42' S, Lon 00° 54' W
The whole part moderate and fair, the wind veering obliged us to tack often to improve it. Kept in soundings from 48 to 62 fathoms.

March 2nd 1741. Woods Hill distance 25 leagues. Lat 50°31' S, Lon 00° 17' W
Continuing our courses to the southward with fair moderate weather, the winds shifting from North West to South West, found soundings from 47 to 50 fathoms, gray sand with small stones.

March 3rd 1741. Woods Hill distance 47 leagues. Lat 51° 15' S, Lon 00° 35' W
The whole part was moderate with several showers of rain in the evening, the later was fair. Directing our course to the southward. Our soundings from 47 to 54 fathoms. In the morning one of the squadron imagined they had seen from the masthead the three Islands of Brothers in the eastward of them.

March 4th 1741. Woods Hill distance 64 leagues. Lat 52° 17' S, Lon 00° 47' W
These 24 hours moderate and fair, the squadron standing to the southward and keeping in soundings from 52 to 30 fathoms, gray sand. At 7 AM. saw land it

being Cape Virgin Mary bearing South by West 10 leagues. This is the western entrance of the Straits of Magellan and is distinguishable by a few round homocks, at the end of a low flat land which runs to the northward of them; but notwithstanding it was very clear could not discern that part of Tierra del Fuego which forms the east side. At 10 AM. the Commodore made the signal for all captains. At noon the Cape bore South West 8 leagues. This day was remarkably clear and warm which gave us some hopes we might meet with tolerable good weather to go round Cape Horn, the squadron being as yet in a reasonable state of health.

March 5th 1741. Woods Hill distance 87 leagues. Lat 53° 36' S, Lon 00° 02' W

The first part little wind and cloudy. At 9 PM. came in with a hard squall of wind and rain, and obliged us to hand our topsails and by 6 in the morning it blew very hard. At 6 PM. Cape Virgin Mary bore 10 leagues; we then had 50 fathoms. From hence we steered south east along the Coast of Tierra del Fuego to Straits Le Maire laying on that point. At 6 AM. were obliged to haul the courses up and steer under our poles, the sloop steering admirably. At 8 the Commodore made the signal to bring to on the starboard tack on which we took 2 reefs in the topsail and lay to in a large hollow sea and had an opportunity of observing the sloop to be an excellent sea boat. At the same time reefed the courses.

March 6th 1741. Woods Hill — 103 leagues. Lat 54° 15' S, Lon 00° 47' W

The first part blew very hard with violent squalls and a sharp cold air, the sea running very hollow. At 11 PM.

the wind abating, the squadron under sail per signal in the southward the wind at the West, we setting our reefed courses and main staysail. At 5 AM. it growing moderate let the reefs out of the courses, and set the topsails. At 8 saw several homocks and mountains, whose tops were covered with snow bearing 9 or 10 leagues; part of Tierra del Fuego. We then sounded and had 46 fathoms, small stones and sand. At noon the southernmost land in sight bore 10 leagues. Tierra del Fuego appeared here in the form of a high broken land its tops covered with snow and near the sea side it looked quite barren and desolate with only a few shrubs on it.

March 7th 1741. Woods Hill distance 103 leagues. Lat 51° 01' S, Lon 01° 06' W

The whole part moderate and fair with smooth water, the wind keeping in the western board. At 4 PM. esteeming ourselves the length of Straits Le Maire brought to per signal on the larboard tack, judging ourselves 6 or 7 leagues off the shore, our soundings from 47 to 50 fathoms, small stones. At 5 AM. the squadron made sail and at 6 discerned the opening of the Straits bearing south 7 leagues, which may be distinguished by 3 mountains called the Three Brothers, having a near resemblance to each other and laying by each other in Tierra del Fuego about 3 miles from the waterside, behind which rose a remarkable single homock much higher than any land near it, and tapering up like a pyramid. At 9 being arrived within 5 miles of the shore the Commodore brought to to wait for the stern-most ships and soon after made sail steering south through the Straits. At our first entrance we had a strong tide which favoured us much till we got half way through, and made such a rippling it resembled breakers. Afterwards we could not observe any tide, either for or against us. We found regular soundings as we sailed through from 45 to 58 fathoms, white sand, the Squadron being nearest to Tierra del Fuego side. At noon were almost through Cape Bartholomew. Staten Land bore 7 leagues, and Cape Good Success on Tierra del Fuego South West 4 leagues; these 2 capes being the entrance of the south part of the Straits.

Off the Straits of Magellan in the first week of March 1741, the ships drifted becalmed, barely moving beneath the dark, ragged cliffs. The officers taking advantage of the lull in the weather came aboard the Centurion on one of those rare peaceful days for an amiable glass of wine and a pleasant talk with the Commodore. The atmosphere, as always, was casual, either in or out of danger. It was the last time all the captains were in company together. Two of them were shortly to vanish and remain unheard of for almost two years, while a third was to be shipwrecked and finally find his way home after five years of amazing adventures.

When the weather suddenly changed the officers hurried back to their ships. The sun became quickly obscured by sinister black clouds as a whining squall struck. The ships heeled to the powerful gusts as they reached through the Le Maire Straits below the terrifying beauty of the overhanging precipices. On one side was the spiny eastern tip of Tierra del Fuego and on the other the monumental spires of Staten Land. The peaks of the mountains on Staten Land were perpetually laden with snow. The Tryall led through the Straits followed by the Centurion, Gloucester, Severn, Pearle, Wager and Anna.

The plan was to pass through the Le Maire Straits and then clear by several hundred miles the southern extremity of Cape Horn. Once through the squadron would head northwest into the Southern Ocean.

CHAPTER SIX: ROUNDING CAPE HORN

The voyage around Cape Horn was to be a nightmare of wild gales that not even the most seasoned sailors of the squadron could anticipate. The Cape, little known at the time, had not been accurately charted in 1741. Narborough had more omissions than details on his charts. Frazier and Halley had made some reasonable plans of Tierra del Fuego but the longitudes were more than 200 miles in error, and Spanish sailing directions were naturally scarce. Those few privateers who had succeeded in rounding the Horn during the winter season recorded but little and praised the Lord that they had survived.

March 9th 1741. Cape Good Success distance 71 leagues. Lat 57° 04' S, Lon 02° 03' W

On board His Majesty's sloop the Tryall. The first part of these 24 hours had a hard squall at west which lasted 2 ½ hours and obliged us to hand our topsails, but being over, set them again. At 6 PM. the southernmost part of Staten Land bore North East 8 leagues. Since we came out of the Straits sounded often but found no ground. The whole squadron since we came through the Straits stood to the southward with the wind variable. At noon saw Staten Land; we judged it North West 12 leagues. We must have had a strong eastern current setting us.

March 10th 1741. Cape Good Success distance 77 leagues. Lat 58° 20' S

The first part moderate with small rain, the middle and latter fresh gales with hard squalls, with much snow and a large hollow sea at AM. Got in the spritsail yard fore and aft to ease the sloop who laboured extremely, and reefed the foresail. At noon had lost sight of the Commodore and squadron, the air being so extremely thick with the large quantities of snow which fell; at the same time had it exceeding cold. Our masts and yards were all crusted over with frozen snow.

March 11th 1741. Cape Good Success distance 75 leagues. Lat 58° 02' S, Lon 03° 59' W

The first part of these 24 hours it continued blowing hard attended with squalls of snow; at 6 PM. the wind abated and it ceased to snow. The air cleared up at ½ past noon, attempted to set the foresail which we had reefed in doing which it split which obliged us to unbend him and bring another to the yard; at 4 PM. had set weather foresail in doing which our men suffered extremely; the vessel frequently rolling them under water as they lay upon the yard; several of them were so benumbed as to be obliged to be helped in; at 6 PM. joined the Commodore and squadron and found our store ship the pink missing who had lost company in the thick weather. At 6 AM. wore ship; at 8 AM. the sea still continuing to run high got the spritsail yard in to ease our bowsprit. The sloop plunging in mightily.

March 12th 1741. Cape Good Success distance 90 leagues. Lat 58° 18' S, Lon 04° 47' W

The first and middle part fresh gales with hard squalls; the latter part grew more moderate; at 4 PM. the Commodore made the signal to speak with us on which we bore down under his lee quarter and received orders from him to keep ahead of the squadron to look out for islands of ice which we began to be apprehensive of, the nights being so extremely obscured that the whole squadron might have been lost on them without some ship ahead to give timely notice of the danger. This night we suffered extremely in the sloop who being obliged to crowd sail to keep the proper distance ahead was almost continually under water; the sea making most of the people who were placed as lookouts out of order, being obliged to keep them in the foretop to look out ahead; the sea running very high. At the daylight joined the squadron; the weather cleared up and grew moderate, but laboured in a large hollow sea. Found by this day's observation the current setting to the northward.

March 13th 1741. Cape Good Success 101 leagues. Lat 58° 59' S, Lon 75° W

These 24 hours proved moderate and fair but the air exceedingly sharp and cold. This evening we were ordered on the Commander's quarter and the Pearle went ahead to look out. The winds continuing in the western board made it very difficult to gain westing. Found the strong northern current setting against us, being by estimation 59° 43' lat and by observation 58° 59' south. Variation by azimuth 24° 48' E.

*March 14th 1741. Cape Good Success 114 leagues. Lat 59°
40' S, Lon 75° 38' W*

Indifferent weather, but often subject to violent squalls
and showers and snow which rendered the air exceeding
cold. The squadron labouring and pitching much in
heading the long hollow swells from the westward. Had
several small birds playing around us called Pintadoes.

*March 15th 1741. Cape Good Success 113 leagues. Lat 58°
48' S, Lon 75° 48' W*

Squally weather with snow, and gloomy and some calms.
At 8 PM. the wind inclining to veer about to the
southward. The Commander made the signal to tack
and stood away with a large head sea. At noon handed
the foretopsail, found a strong northern current setting
against us which rendered us dubious of our westing, it
not being improbable the current may likewise set to the
eastward round Cape Horn and so discharge itself
through the Straits of Le Maire.

*March 16th 1741. Cape Good Success 118 leagues. Lat 59°
25' S, Lon 75° 32' W*

Squally, tempestuous weather with hail. At 1 PM. tacked
per signal and stood to the southward; at 6 AM. saw a
sail to the eastward on which the Commodore made the
Gloucester signal to chase, the whole squadron likewise
standing after her. Brought her to, and found her to be
the pink our store ship who had lost company with us
sometime before.

March 17th 1741. Cape Good Success 138 leagues. Lat 59° 49' S, Lon 77° 12' W

Fresh gales with thick hazy weather. At 2 PM. took in main topsails. At 6 handed them both; the squalls being very violent with heavy showers of rain; about 10 in the evening the weather cleared up and proved moderate for the remaining part. AM. set the main topsail.

March 18th 1741. Cape Good Success 139 leagues. Lat 58° 27' S, Lon 79° 18' W

Uncertain weather frequently intermixed with hard squalls attended with much snow and an irregular chopping sea which often broke all over us and obliged us to ply both our pumps all night.

March 19th 1741. Cape Good Success 138 leagues. Lat 57° 25' S, Lon 81° 06' W

The whole part squally with snow. AM. set the foretopsail at 11 tacked per signal. The wind veered about and died. Our people much began to grow sickly and impatient at the long run of tempestuous weather, the short time the southerly wind lasted having gave us hopes to soon have run to the northward and bettered our climate, instead the wind obliged us to tack and stand back to the southward again.

March 21st 1741. Cape Good Success 108 leagues. Lat 56° 18' S, Lon 83° 39' W

Moderate with some showers of sleet and snow and a great western sea. About noon it began to blow fresh with heavy squalls with very large hail. Were in great hopes of a south west wind which would finally permit us to run to the northward, our men over all the squadron much afflicted with the scurvy.

March 22nd 1741. Cape Good Success 176 leagues. Lat 56° 09' S, Lon 84° 18' W
Stormy weather with violent squalls and hail. The weather very cold and uncomfortable, our people being continually wet and much harrassed and jaded. At 9 PM. tacked per signal, the wind veering back to the north quarter and stood to the southward.

March 23rd 1741. Cape Good Success 172 leagues. Lat 56° 58' S, Lon 83° 43' W
Blew very hard with a large hollow sea breaking continually over us; our masts and rigging all coated with frozen snow and ice. At 1 PM. the squadron brought to with their heads to the southward. We brailled our trysail and lay to; about 2 in the morning the wind abated and the weather cleared up. At 10 made sail to the south west.

March 24th 1741. Cape Good Success 177 leagues. Lat 57° 25' S, Lon 83° 43'W
Much squally weather with rain. At 4 PM. handed the maintopsail and brailled the trysail; night looking very dismal. At 9 PM. a violent squall came on being then under topsail, main staysail and brailled trysail which lay the sloop almost under water. At the same time we were close on by one of the 50 gun ships on his weather beam and had the pink close to us to windward, who in the violence of the squall was bearing away before it and very near on board of us. I was obliged to depend on

her wearing which she providentially performed and brushed close under the 50 gun ship stern. Having thus escaped hauled the foresail up and lay to under bare poles to the northward. At 12 the fiercest of the gales abating discerned one of our ships laying to the south, on which we wore and lay the same way. At 4 AM. saw the Commodore's light which we had lost in the first of the night. The sloop hauled, being half-full of water with the seas which we had shipped and were obliged to keep bailing and pumping all night, our pumps being likewise but very indifferent, being continually choked up with sand.

March 25th 1741. Cape Good Success 184 leagues. Lat 57° 41' S, Lon 84° 50' W

Uncertain squally weather; the latter part blew exceptionally hard with much hail. Got our anchors in upon deck to ease our bows, the sloop labouring much and struck all our swivel guns off the decks. At 10 AM. we were obliged to haul the foresail up and lay to not being able to carry sail any longer; being in danger of foundering and thereby lost sight of the squadron.

March 26th 1741. Cape Good Success 178 leagues. Lat 58° 05' S, Lon 84° 10' W

Hard gale, the latter moderate and fair. At 6 PM. it clearing up saw the Commander and the squadron laying to the southward of us, on which we bore down and joined them, and brought to. AM. made sail with the squadron to the southward.

March 27th 1741. Cape Good Success

Moderate with hazy weather and rain. At 11 AM. tacked and stood to to the northward being very desirous of getting northing and began to hope we had got sufficiently to the westward of Cape Horn to double it and stand for the Southern Sea.

Demoralised and sick, the crew of the Tryall hoped for a change in the wind that would allow them to sail west and north and thereby pass safely around Cape Horn and enter the Southern Ocean. Constant tacking and lying-to against fierce head winds had made any accurate calculation of their position impossible. At the end of March the wind direction changed which briefly lifted the spirits of the sailors.

March 31st 1741. Cape Good Success 216 leagues. Lat 57° 12'S, Lon 88° W

Moderate and cloudy; began to entertain hopes that the southern winds would prevail and carry us clear of the Cape. At 2 PM. the Gloucester's main yard broke short off in the slings. This obliged the whole squadron to bring to and assist her with carpenters from each ship. Thus by some accident or other we were always prevented from improving a fair wind. At 5 received a hand pump from the Commodore, the sloop being very bad. The squadron lay to the whole of the night till the Gloucester had rigged a main topsail yard for a main yard and at 7 AM. the squadron made an easy sail to the northward with the wind at the south west.

April 1st 1741. Cape Good Success 215 leagues. Lat 56° 07' S, Lon 88° W

Moderate with dark cloudy weather. Towards the latter part began to freshen with squalls and rain, the squadron making an easy sail to the northward.

April 2nd 1741. Cape Good Success 214 leagues. Lat 54° 38' S, Lon 87° 18' W

Fresh gales with hail and rain and a great sea. 5 PM. handed the topsail; at noon handed the main topsail. The weather inclinable to return to the northern board.

April 3rd 1741. Cape Good Success 215 leagues. Lat 54° 46' S, Lon 88° 07' W

Fresh gales with hard squalls; a great hollow sea. 6 PM. the wind being to the north west the Commodore made the signal to wear and stand to the westward and handed main topsail. At 3 PM. the squadron brought to per signal, it blowing so excessive hard as rendered it impractical to keep one's sides up to it.

April 4th 1741. Cape Good Success 214 leagues. Lat 54° 44 S, Lon 87° 57' W

Fresh gales with more violent squalls and rainy; the latter part the weather began to be more moderate and cleared up. 9 AM. the whole squadron made sail to the northward with the wind at northwest. Set up our courses and main topsail.

April 5th 1741. Cape Good Success 193 leagues. Lat 55° 21' S, Lon 87° 44' W

Blew very hard with a great sea with violent squalls of hail which rendered it extremely cold. The sloop labouring and taking much water. At 2 PM. handed the main topsail and at 4 PM. the squadron brought to to the westward per signal. At noon made sail to the south west quarter.

April 6th 1741. Cape Good Success 207 leagues. Lat 55° 47' S, Lon 88° 45' W
Moderate and cloudy. At 1 PM. set main topsail, found the variation 22°E. The latter part thick foggy weather.

April 7th 1741. Cape Good Success 207 leagues. Lat 55° 54' S, Lon 88° 45' W
Fresh gales and hazy first part, the middle and latter blew hard with showers and rain. A great sea with a cold air. At 4 PM. the Commander made the signal to bring to on the starboard tack.

April 8th 1741. Cape Good Success 205 leagues. Lat 55° 54' S, Lon 88° 39' W
Fresh gales, dark cloudy weather. At 9 PM. the Commander made sail with the squadron to the westward. At 6 he made the signal to the squadron to keep close with each other to prevent separation at night time. At 9 PM. wore per signal, the wind shifting to the south west. At 4 PM. the Commander made the signal to bring to on the starboard tack, the Wager having made the signal of distress and at daylight found she had lost her mizzen mast, her iron work giving way. At 9 made sail again to the northward.

April 9th 1741. Cape Good Success 191 leagues. Lat 55° 07' S, Lon 87° 03' W

Gales and new squalls with rain. At 4 PM. the store ship made the signal of distress at which the Commander bore down to him found his forestay broke and gammoning, and his bowsprit in great danger. At noon the Commander made the signal to wear and stand to to the westward the wind having shifted to the northward.

April 10th 1741. Cape Good Success 212 leagues. Lat 55° 41' S, Lon 88° 58' W

Later it blew fresh squalls. At daylight found the Severn and Pearle missing who had lost company in the night and probably fell astern by not carrying so much sail as the rest of the squadron. At 10 PM. it fell calm, the sloop labouring much in a large hollow sea. At noon a small breeze coming up the Commander made the signal to wear and had to stand to the northward.

For a few brief days during the middle of April the weather turned moderate and there was respite from the incessant storms. The ships, periodically driven from their formation in the gales or lost in the fog, somehow managed, despite broken rigging and scurvy, to re-unite as they tacked back and forth against the prevailing northern winds, fighting to clear the Horn. The Severn and Pearle had not been seen for several weeks and the Commodore, while not giving the ships up for lost, did not expect to see them again until the next rendezvous was reached at the island of Socorro on the south Chilean coast.

At Staten Land in March the deceptively warm weather had given the squadron false hopes for an easy passage. Saumarez prematurely began 'to look on the conquest of the Peruvian mines and principal towns of the Pacific as an amusement which would naturally occur. But from this time forward we met with nothing but disasters and accidents. Never were the passions of hope and fear so much exercised; the very elements seemed combined against us. I had to endure such fatigues from the severity of the weather, and the duty which the nature and charge of the sloop brought upon me, that really life is not worth preserving at the expense of such hardships.'

April 13th 1741. Cape Good Success 214 leagues. Lat 54° 36' S, Lon 78° 46' W

Cape Noir by my accounts lay 78° 46' W, finding it by most correct draughts I could get to lay 09° W off the Straits Le Maire. By my accounts was 9° 30' too westerly. Some were still more. The currents having thus far deceived us with our frequent laying to and shortening sail. Squally. At 1 AM. providentially clearing up discerned land right ahead about 2 leagues making like an island with 2 homocks and by my observation was probably an island called Cape Noir laying off the Straits of Magellan. This was a most unexpected sight, esteeming ourselves at that time near 200 leagues off. Most authors who have sailed this way have indeed cautioned against a strong eastern current, but from our westing which we imagined as considerable as any who have sailed this way we were in hopes at last to have weathered the Straits of Magellan which lay 72° 15' W. The Commander immediately made the signal to stand to the South West, the wind being then at West North West. We sounded and found 60 fathoms at 6 AM. The same land bore north.

We now know that sailing instructions given to Commodore Anson were wrong, and that in April in 1741 the western gales blew almost unceasingly.

By this time Anson could assess the calibre of his officers. Under stress their true characters quickly emerged. Certain men stood out as the voyage progressed. Charles Saunders was proving to be a capable officer while Peircy Brett, a competent artist and draughtsman, was also a man of considerable courage. Augustus van Keppel (son of the Duke of Richmond), midshipman, barely sixteen when they reached the Horn, displayed a coolness under danger and a responsibility that would soon be rewarded.

Edward Legge of the Severn and George Murray of the Pearle turned back after several unsuccessful attempts to round the Cape and ran off before the gales to the River Plate, eventually reaching Rio de Janiero. Their crews were no more disabled than the crews of the other ships, and they would have been no worse off had they remained with the squadron. The presence of two more fighting ships in the Pacific might have changed the course of history for Britain. Anson at the time presumed the Severn and Pearle had been lost. Their commanders' reasons for returning were irrefutable. It seemed that they simply could not go on. They had reached the end. In fact there was no plausible reason for anyone continuing beyond the Horn in the face of more certain destruction. Except that brave men differed. Under the ultimate test Anson had a will that could not be weakened by adversity. So had Saumarez. Those fine, slight differences in human nature, never quite apparent until the final crisis, now showed themselves among the men. Colonel Cracherode, colonel of a dying force of marines, also clung grimly to life. He was a battered veteran of a dozen wars and survived to lead his pitiful remnants against the Spaniards at Payta in Chile. After Anson himself, the character of Philip Saumarez dominated. Perhaps the quiet, tortured nature of the man had been inhibited too long in the rigid cast of the Navy, and at last Anson gave Saumarez the chance he wanted. In many ways the rounding of Cape Horn in the Tryall was the making of Saumarez.

For over a month the squadron attempted to gain the west coast of Patagonia and leave behind the bleak, wild isthmus of Tierra del Fuego. The isthmus projected like a curved beak on the extremity of South America, bent back by untold centuries of severe storms. Master Justinian Nutt, the chief navigator of the squadron who served aboard the Centurion, had allowed for double the leeway that all former expeditions had calculated in their passage around the Horn. But this was insufficient. Following the advice of former navigators, the squadron had stood to the south to keep well clear of the coastal tides and currents. In the conflicting streams and winds the ships were flung about like small boats. One man on the Centurion broke a collar bone, several fractured their legs and arms, while two seamen were thrown overboard and lost. From March to May there were almost continuous storms on an unprecedented scale.

Water constantly flooded the decks of all the ships, especially the Tryall, straining ahead of the squadron with the seas cascading like waterfalls from the plunging bows. Towards the middle of April, 'there came a storm, which both in its violence and continuation exceeded all that we had hitherto encountered'. It lasted three days. On the last day the quarter gallery of the Centurion near the poop was stove in and water 'rushed into the ship like a deluge'. Shrouds broke and for days the Centurion lay under bare poles, heaving and crashing helplessly into the seas until the storm gradually subsided.

On April 14 Saumarez on a signal from the Commodore bore down on his quarter to receive new orders. Saunders was now recovered from his illness and was to relieve him of command of the Tryall. Saumarez was to return to duty as Anson's first officer aboard the Centurion. After coming on board the Centurion Saumarez was appalled at what he found. Almost everyone was infected with the scurvy and badly demoralised. Forty men had been lost since they came through the Le Maire Straits and most of the crew were unable to perform their duties. On each watch no more than 70 seamen could be mustered, while the marines were all either sick or dead.

April 16th 1741. Cape Good Success 218 leagues. Lat 56° 18' S, Lon 81° 04' W
Fresh gales with hard squalls. At 7 PM. the wind returned to the North West and made the signal to wear and stand to at noon. John Deland and John Parker seamen deceased. Joseph Owens and John Williams soldier died.

April 17th 1741. Cape Good Success 228 leagues. Lat 57° 18' S, Lon 81° 30' W
Fresh gales with hard squalls, the most part with a sharp cold air. At 8 PM. a hard squall coming on broke the main sheet but pulling the main sail briskly up saved the sail having fixed it again at 9 PM. At 10 set the main topsail. George Ramsey seaman, Francis Sullivan and George Ruth soldiers departed this life.

*April 18th 1741. Cape Good Success 235 leagues. Lat 58° 21'
S, Lon 82° 33' W*

The weather somewhat more moderate, but subject to
squalls attended by hail. At 2 PM. reaching away with
the whole squadron southward hoping to get a
favourable wind to double the Cape and Straits of
Magellan. Allan Ellison and Ref. Roberts marines,
deceased.

*April 22nd 1741. Cape Good Success 257 leagues. Lat 59° 26'
S, Lon 84° 38' W*

Winds from the South. Today fresh gales the latter
squally with snow. At 9 PM. the wind shifting to the
southward made the signal to wear estimating ourselves
in 60° 28' S. It was surprising to observe what effect our
different tacks had on the spirits of our people generally.
The sick revived and grew better whenever we stood to
the North and had prospect of getting round.

*April 23rd 1741. Cape Good Success 114 leagues. Lat 58° 01'
S, Lon 86° 06' W*

The first part blew fresh with squalls of snow and hail.
The latter proving more moderate with some intervals
of calms and sunshine which we used in repairing and
setting up our rigging which was broken and shattered
and took the tarpaulins off our gratings and hatchways
to air between decks and clean the ship as much as lay in
our power; and really it is scarce conceivable what a
stench and nastyness our poor sick people had caused
among each other and which contributed to infect those
who struggled against distemper.

*April 24th 1741. Cape Good Success 123 leagues. Lat 57° 10'
S, Lon 87° 58' W*

The first part calm, the middle began to grow fresh with
very thick weather and the latter part blew a hard storm.
The wind shifting and attended with a dangerous hollow
sea; at 5 PM. the wind springing up made an easy sail to
the westward under topsails, with the squadron round
us, but growing thick weather soon lost sight of them,
but continued our way with such an easy sail as we
judged might keep them company; at 5 AM. the wind
increasing attempted to hand the main topsail but being
at the time weakly manned and the clew lines and
buntlines breaking and the sheets half flown and the sail
soon split, and by its violent shakings endangering the
head of the mast we were obliged to cut him from the
yard. At 8 brought to to hand the foresails, but then at
the first shake split and beat about the yard in such a
manner as rendered it impracticable to go out and hand
him; it soon beat to pieces. Our mainsail at the time
blowing loose and the clew grommets, buntlines and
leech lines breaking were obliged to lower the yard
down to secure the sail. On lowering the fore-yard down
likewise the ship falling broad off in the hollow of the
seas laboured exceedingly, taking prodigious deep rolls
and shipped a great quantity of water. At noon had no
sight of the squadron.

The ships were now in another terrible storm. While the
weather continued to take its toll of the gear, the scurvy
continued to take its toll of men. It was now, as it would be
again, a question of what hidden resources the leaders and men
of the expedition could call upon for survival. Fortunately, the

weather suddenly improved.

On April 27 the Wager fired a signal of distress. The storm had pulled her rigging ironwork from the hull, and her mizzen mast having no shrouds to support it toppled onto the deck. The following day the Anna fired a distress signal. Her forestay had parted and there was danger 'of all her mast coming by the board'. Temporary repairs were arranged on the two ships as the rest of the squadron hove-to until all could continue again.

April 27th 1741. Cape Good Success 147 leagues. Lat 53° 25' S, Lon 90° 35' W

Fair weather. Set up all our shrouds and back stays and fitted our rigging up against the next storm. Richard Dolby and Robert Hood seamen and William Thompson marine deceased. Set the topsails. Our men now began to decline a pace, the scurvy reigning among us and making terrible havoc.

April 28th 1741. Cape Good Success 160 leagues. Lat 53° 12' S, Lon 91° 19' W

Winds from the West North West more favourable. Tolerable good weather the whole part, but often threatening with black heavy clouds. 5 PM. and at daylight set the topsails again; were now so enfeebled by the loss and sickness of our men that we were obliged to carry sail with all the precaution imaginable not being strong enough to hand them in case of wind; at 1 PM. wore and stood to the westward and found by this day's work a current setting to the southward. Robert Pierce, John Mell, seamen deceased.

Aboard the Tryall after Saunders took command on April 14,

there were no more than the captain, lieutenant, purser, surgeon and two boys 'to work the sloop, mend the sails, bury the dead and do the more servile offices.' All the crews ate mainly bread, toasted over brandy to kill the vermin that infested the food. Sails were blown out for want of strength to bring them in. Seamen in the last stages of scurvy gave themselves up to the fatal, hopeless depression that killed quickly. 'And we only used to envy those whose good fortune it was to die first.' Water was rationed to less than two pints a day. It was estimated that on a dead man there was at least a peck of lice, and all the ships were infested with vermin.

On May 8 the Centurion reached the rendezvous off the island of Nuestra Señora de Socorro, but no one else had arrived. All Saumarez could see on the barren mainland coastline was giant breakers crashing on the shore, and although there might be a hidden anchorage somewhere nearby it was unwise to sail too close to the coast in these uncharted waters while large seas were running.

The sick crew of the Centurion cruised the area waiting for the arrival of the squadron. When no one appeared after a week the Centurion sailed to the alternative rendezvous at Chiloe Island, 150 miles to the north. But the sea did not show any kindness to the sick crew and the battered ship. If it were still possible, a storm wilder than all those which had come before descended, 'in which the fury of all the storms which we had hitherto encountered seemed to be combined and to have conspired our destruction', and every newly sewn sail was split by the wind.

May 12th 1741. The Island of Succoro on the coast of Chile 55 leagues. Lat 46° 05' S, Lon 82° 55' W
More gales. Weather very uncertain. At 4 PM. handed the topsails. At 6 PM. the wind shifting to the North

West wore ship and stood to the eastward. John MacMannus, man-at-arms, deceased. Our ship's company was in most deplorable condition, the distemper gaining ground on our people daily.

May 13th 1741. Island of Succoro 63 leagues. Lat 46° 27' S, Lon 83° 20' W
Gales, rain and squalls on this day with a large hollow sea. As we stood to our main sheet broke which obliged us to haul the clew garnet up, the leech line giving way likewise lowered the mainyard down to save the sail and lay to under foresail. At 10 AM. attempted to wear ship but the foresail splitting brought another and reset him and made sail to the northward. Arthur James, Vernon Head seamen deceased. The latter died suddenly.

There seemed little prospect of meeting any ships of the squadron at Chiloe, so Anson gave orders to immediately sail another 700 miles north to Juan Fernandez, his only hope of salvation. They had to reach the island to save what was left of the ship and men.

May 17th 1741. The south end of the Island of Chiloe, the Island of Guaffo 12 leagues. Lon 79° 55' W
A continuation of stormy surprising weather, the elements seeming all confused. In the height of the squall had several violent claps of thunder; before the explosion of which a quick subtle fire ran along our decks which bursting made a report like a pistol and struck several of our men and officers who with the violence of the blow were black and blue in several places. This fire was attended with a strong sulphurous

smell; at 4 PM. our fore sheet broke which endangered splitting the sail but clearing it but briskly saved him and reeved a new one; at 5 PM. clearing up saw a small island which we took to be the island of Guaffo bearing East by South 10 leagues. The wind blowing directly on gave us apprehension of our being drove on it, the sea riding very high. At 12 PM. the winds shifting to the West North West wore ship being afraid of being drove between the islands of Chiloe which we judged to be 10 leagues asunder. At 3 PM. were taken aback with a squall, the ship refusing to wear and our people not strong enough to haul the sail up, lowered down the main yard. At 7 AM. the wind abating encouraged our hands to bend the main topsail and set him close reefed with which difficulty was performed, being able to muster about 27 men, our people being dispirited and fatigued beyond what can be imagined; at 8 it clearing up a short time, discerned the looming up of the land about South East of us. At noon saw a high bluff of land East of us which we imagined to be the southernmost end of Chiloe. By what we can observe the island Chiloe seems to run about NBW and SBE and the island of Guaffo to lay to the westward of it. Else we should scarce have weathered Chiloe, the charts laying the two islands near north and south of each other. Erroneously placed.

May 23rd 1741. The middle of the Island of Chiloe 43 leagues. Lat 43° 08' S, Lon 82° 22' W
Hard gales and very thick weather. 6 PM. blew a violent storm in the northward, continued until 8 PM. and finding it coming on handed the main topsail and kept

her away larking to prevent the loss of our mast. At 7 shipped a very dangerous sea on the quarter which gave us a prodigious shock; at 12 PM. the wind was much abated but laboured in a hollow overgrown sea. At 8 AM. it fell calm. Upon overhauling our rigging found that last night we had broken three of the starboard main shrouds, three of the lanyards of the starboard fore ones, and two of the larboard side. The ship rolling endangered our mast considerably, the fore mast particularly, who was scarce supported by any rigging and fetched much. With difficulty we wore her in order to head to sea to prevent her rolling and set the main topsail to steady her; at noon the wind shifted at once to the southward and threatened another storm from that quarter which made us hand the main topsail, but our people were now so weak and dispirited that it was with much difficulty performed. Set the foresail to wear the ship, in doing which we split him. However, we kept the ship afore it with our mainsail set and really she steered exceedingly well. Thos. Walker and Wm. Ward seamen, deceased. Found the ship to heel 3 strakes to port occasioned by the shock of the sea which we received, our cables being settled over with several things in the hold.

May 24th 1741. Middle of the Island of Chiloe 60 leagues. Lat 41° S, Lon 82° 39' W

Squally with rain, the middle and latter moderate and fair. Found by this day's reckoning that the island is 15 mins. more northerly than we thought. PM. lowered the fore yard down to mend it, the foresail which being done at 4 swayed him up again. AM. employed in repairing our rigging which was all broken. James Casten and John Shepherd soldiers deceased.

May 25th 1741. Middle of the Island of Chiloe 92 leagues. Lat 39° 12' S, Lon 82° 50' W
Fresh gales and fair. Got up new fore topmast backstays; running away to the northward with joyful hearts in hopes to mend our climate, and really it was time. Most of our men being now so sick that we did not muster above 20 seamen in each watch. At the same time our sick dying a pace. AM. set the foretopsail. Several strange creatures swimming about us which we took to be sea lions; an exceeding sharp subtle air. 5 more men died including one midshipman.

May 26th 1741. Middle of the Island of Chiloe 140 leagues. Lat 37° 20' S, Lon 85° 12' W
Fresh gales, some showers of rain. Going away to the northward found the weather considerably softer and most of the birds which had followed us began to leave us. They kept us company ever since we came through the Straits. 4 more seamen deceased.

Towards the end of May they were sailing away from the storms. Though their correct latitude was known there was no way of calculating accurate longitudes at sea. They could be either to the west or the east of their destination. Since their dead reckoning position was unsure it was a guess where Juan Fernandez lay.

Longitude is an east-west measurement of position as opposed to latitude, which is a north-south measurement of position. Once out of sight of land, Saumarez could only find his latitude from the noon sight, a system which had been in use for many centuries. A longitude sight required accurate timing from a chronometer, and Harrison's chronometer was yet to be perfected, tested and made generally available. The method of lunar distances was used on the expedition, mainly to fix the positions of islands, etc. However, because of its complexity, and because the accuracy required in the observations was far greater than for latitude sights, it was rarely used at sea at that time. Longitudes were determined on land by this method, as is noted elsewhere in Saumarez's account.

Sir

I am convinced you will readilly assent that an ambition when pursued by laudable methods of serving one's Country by raising to parts of greater trust and confidence, is what the most rigid virtue and honour encourages; this granted will serve as an attonement for the intrusion of these lines which you will receive as the expostulations of a person who since his first admission to the honour of receiving your command has employed all his facilities and made it his principal study to deserve a place in your esteem and obtain from you the character of being a good officer. How far I have succeeded must be referred to you. My own jealousy's suggest to me a very indifferent prospect in a point I have so reddilly pursued. Nor will you censure me as entertaining vain scruples, if you permitt me to reflect on the delays which prevented you employing your victory over the common enemy in regard to ourselves. Is to my owne part what I gather from your last conversation was allways foreign to my thoughts. Nor was it ever my intentions to enter into competitions with the interests of a person I flattered my self to esteem as my benefactor. In this point I am ready to give you what assurances you will think, necessary to receive. In other circumstance which gives me the utmost concern is your intentions of superseding me by another Officer. This distinction which I forbear calling invidious in regard to me you omitted with my other two predecessors. I came out of this with Captain Cheap as your immediate officers, I hoped at least to have shared the same run of fortune, there was then no conditionall preferment given, but permit me to mention one incidence, when you indulged me with the charge of the Tryall Sloop round Cape Horn, and if any thing might have given room for some reversion of preferment in my favour, but the event was quite contrary from the period of time and date my having last grown in your esteem, and as to Capt. Saunders it never entered in his thoughts to make me the least compliment as if he had never recollected that in the extremity of weather we underwent, I had at best as plausible a reason to have separated and bore up as the rest of your squadron did. In what regards of discharge of my duty I am far from arrogating to my self the least merritt and as to any opportunities I may ever have of your esteem and regard I have ever entertained for you, to favour me with your belief, yet no one will embrace you with more cheerfullness. Is these are the results of my thoughts I could not forbear in the fullness of my mind to insert it, I can as little forbear troubling you with, now whatever be your success be persuaded my resolutions shall ever be first and determined to profit and subscribe my self with the profoundest respect of

Your most obedient
Humble servant
PS

May 28th 1741. Island of Chiloe 197 leagues. Lat 33° 55' S, Lon 84° 08' W

Moderate and fair — looked out all night for the island of Juan Fernandez imagining ourselves near the meridian. AM. being in the parallel of latitude and having no sight of it began to suspect our draughts might be erroneous which lay it down at the same meridian as the island of Chiloe, but others lay it down a bit to the Westward. Conceiving we had sufficient westing hauled up to the East by North intending to keep in the parallel of 33° 30' S in hopes of making of it soon. Two more seamen died and three soldiers. Variation 9° 48' E.

May 29th 1741. Island of Chiloe 189 leagues. Lat 33° 55' S, Lon 81° 44' W

Moderate and clear. Had all our faculties awake to look out for the island, our people being grown to the last degree infirm and sick and few of them able to do their duty, falling down hourly. AM. seeing no sight of land began to give it up, and concluded we had not had sufficient westing, but bounding Cape Horn were now gone to the eastward of it, but as this thing was uncertain continued our course to the eastward knowing we must either fall in with it soon or make the Continent, from which we should take a fresh departure and clear up all our doubts. 6 more people died. Several of these men were strong enough to crawl upon the deck to breath the fresh air and bask in the sun but no sooner had they come but they fainted away and soon were expired, though at the first coming into the sun they expressed great satisfaction in being on the deck. Found one of our main and fore shrouds broke which we new stoppered. Found the variation to be 8 deg. 48 min. east.

May 30th 1741. Island of Chiloe 189 leagues. Lat 33° 55' S, Lon 80° W

By this run from the Island of Chiloe it is evident the coast runs from the latitude of 42° 14' S to 33° 55' S.

Runs nearest north and south. At 11 AM. saw the Continent to the East. We judged ourselves about 10 or 12 leagues off, nor would we venture near lest we should have been discovered by some of the watchmen. The land was exceeding high and uneven appearing quite white — this might be probably the Cordilleros who are always covered with snow, and lay a great way inland. We observed several spots like islands which no doubt were the tops of mountains near the sea side just rising out of the water. 2 seamen and one soldier deceased.

The Centurion should have reached Juan Fernandez on May 28, but for the above reasons Saumarez could not calculate his longitude and position. Justinian Nutt, the master responsible for navigation, had erred on several vital occasions before. He had been out 300 miles on the shores of Patagonia, and this time he had wrongly suggested they follow their latitude east to the coast of Chile and this way run down on the island. For two days they had an easy run before a following breeze eastward, but when they saw the Chilean coast they realised that Nutt had chosen the wrong direction, and had to struggle all the way back against the wind to the west. The error cost the Centurion a hundred dead from scurvy, but possibly saved the ship for a Spanish expedition had been waiting at Juan Fernandez for the squadron until a few days before the Centurion arrived. The Spaniards had orders to put every Englishman to the sword but they had tired of waiting and left for the mainland. In their weakened condition the English sailors could not have put up much resistance.

June 8th 1741 Part of the Coast of Chile last seen 93 leagues. Lat 33° 43' S, Lon 85° 26' W

At the break of day discovered the larger of the two islands of Juan Fernandez 11 or 12 leagues, the wind being then at North, appearing like a high broken mountainous island. This was a joyful sight to us who were now reduced to an exceeding weakness. At 9 tacked and stood to the eastward. At noon the island bore north 10 leagues.

The following day the Centurion edged towards the island with Saumarez at the helm assisted by six seamen and two junior masters of the watch. The only other assistance available to work the vessel came from officers and servants. It took them two hours to wear ship, a manoeuvre that normally took twenty minutes with a full crew. Eleven seamen and soldiers had been buried that day.

CHAPTER SEVEN: THE SHIPWRECK OF THE WAGER

When the Wager under command of Captain Cheap parted company with the Centurion on April 24 she sailed northward, struggling against the same gales that battered the other ships of the squadron. The captain, who carried aboard the field artillery for the proposed assault on Valdivia, intended to rendezvous at the island of Nuestra Señora de Socorro with the Commodore as planned.

In mid-April the Wager had lost her mizzen mast and most of her main shrouds. In early May all the fore halyard blocks parted so that it was no longer possible to use any foresails. Under jury rig she might have been able to still make Juan Fernandez in the more favourable winds that blew during May and June and which allowed the Anna to arrive at that island. But Cheap did not seem to possess the same iron will of many of the other officers, and with the disappearance of the Centurion the paternal authority of Anson, which was always a mighty source of strength, was gone.

Cheap had little knowledge of the Gulf of Penas on the Patagonia coast and his charts did not cover any area in detail. The Wager carried a crew of 243 men out of which 132 were marines, most of whom were dead. Three-quarters of the remainder were sick from scurvy. By the time the lee shore was observed on May 14 no more than six men could be mustered on the watch to man the 560 ton ship. Cheap was in a state of bewilderment. Land should have been visible only to the east off the starboard bow. Instead he saw land to port, and to starboard was the shore towards which the boat was drifting, making considerable leeway without the help of either foresails or mizzen. Unknown to the crew they were trapped between the Peninsular de Tres Montes, a westward projection of the Continent, and the coast of Patagonia. They were being set into the Gulf of Penas in mountainous seas with a full gale blowing out of the west.

The lassitude induced by illness was further aggravated by the obtuseness of Cheap, who refused to heed the warnings of his officers and men who were aware of the impending disaster. Cheap thought the shore he approached was Socorro although he was a good 300 miles south of it. In a final panic Cheap tried to drive his crew to set more sail to claw off the land. Although they managed to change the direction of the ship's head to the west she continued to drift almost due south. In the fearful commotion Cheap slipped on deck and badly dislocated his shoulder and was confined at a critical time to the surgeon's cabin.

Every sail was torn, much of the rigging unsecured, when at 4.50 am on May 15 the ship struck a submerged rock. However, she drifted off again, badly holed, her rudder immobilised, and finally lodged between two giant boulders as dawn broke. Land was not far away and by unlashing the small boats most of the men made shore. Those few who were left aboard became roaring drunk on brandy ransacked from the ship's stores. The negligence and unreasoning stubbornness of their captain was to set the stage for eventual mutiny.

Cheap proved incapable of dealing with the situation. The gunner, Bulkely, from the moment he stepped ashore became the natural leader of the 140 men marooned on the beach. After a week starvation and exposure to the bitter cold of Patagonia was taking a steady toll of lives. The haughty mannerisms of Cheap, who managed to impose by force alone some small measure of authority, alienated all but a few officers. When Cheap, in a fit of violent temper, shot Midshipman Cozens for insulting behaviour, the survivors had already formed an opposing group to defy the authority of the captain.

The unexpected appearance of small bands of Indians who bartered a little food with the sailors saved them all from immediate starvation. The few stores that were salvaged from the ship had to be carefully guarded against theft. Every man lived in a state of continual semi-starvation, bickering constantly. The survivors eventually formed small gangs foraging for shellfish, wild fowl, herbs or any stray dogs that found their way into what had become known as Wager Island. On one occasion a band of 50 Indians brought some sheep and seafood and after a short stay departed when their women were molested. Boat trips to the wreck for food and provisions yielded less on each successive journey.

Meanwhile, work was going ahead on the longboat under supervision of the carpenter, to increase its length to 50 feet. The plan was then to sail the longboat and cutter south through the Straits of Magellan with about 80 men until the Rio Grande in Brazil was reached.

But an unbearable tension was building up between Cheap on one hand and the remarkable Bulkely and his men on the other. Bulkely refused to accept Cheap as a competent leader. One day Bulkely presented a written petition to Cheap: the longboat, which was almost complete, must for the common good sail through the Magellan Straits, while Cheap insisted it was his duty to rendezvous with Anson at Socorro or Valdivia in the north. John Young, a cooper and one of the future mutineers, observed 'these disputes and Civilities were equally insignificant; the contending parties were neither reciprocally convinced nor reconciled'. Cheap had all but lost control, only permitted to rule by Bulkely under tolerance. Cheap tried to find support for his cause with bribes of liquor. John Young noted that 'the Gunner and Carpenter were mightily alarmed at this, supposing the Captain had spirited up a party against their scheme, which they regarded as a kind of subornation of Treason against his Sovereign, the People'.

Early in October after weeks of indecision, Bulkeley's group with the approval of some of the officers arrested Cheap, who was to be marooned on Wager Island by an amazing mutual agreement. On October 13 the lengthened longboat, christened the Speedwell, was launched and John Young saw themselves 'embarked, entering on our important voyage, all of us stocked with eager desire, feeble hopes and gloomy apprehensions'. The 'People' had taken the right course. By October the remains of the squadron who had arrived at Juan Fernandez had left and were off to Mexico. There would have been no chance of meeting the ships had the Wager's survivors headed north under Cheap.

Behind on Wager Island Bulkeley left the captain, the surgeon and Midshipman Hamilton. The parting between Bulkeley and Cheap had been strangely cordial, almost tearful: 'to hear Bulkeley's moving account you would have thought he was painting the last Separation of David and Jonathon.' Bulkeley had the presence of mind in the circumstances to draw up an astutely worded petition signed by all hands, which endorsed his actions.

Provisions for Cheap and the others were left on the beach, including ample supplies of arms and ammunition. As she departed the Speedwell's crew shouted three loud cheers for the men they left behind. After two days the barge which had accompanied the longboat returned to Cheap at Wager Island with Midshipman the Honourable John Byron, and four men who had second thoughts after experiencing a taste of the boat's dreadfully cramped quarters. But the cutter still accompanied the Speedwell and throughout the journey Bulkeley, somehow or other in the wet, hive-like congestion, kept a journal.

On October 31, 1741 Bulkeley found a sandy bay for anchorage where 'we shot wild geese in abundance and got of shellfish, as limpets and mussels'. On November 3 they lost the cutter, which broke adrift, and were unable to find her again. Henceforth they could not go ashore for food and had to use what was left of the hard rations. Ten men were put 'voluntarily' on the beach to ease the overloading aboard Speedwell before the Straits were entered. In the Straits of Magellan the boat was on several occasions broached by mountainous seas, swamped and almost smashed on the rocks. 'We have several times very narrowly escaped being made a Wreck and sometimes have been preserved when we have seen our Fate before our eyes and every moment expected it, when all the conduct and ability of men could have availed nothing.'

On December 26 they miraculously passed through the Straits of Magellan and reached Cape Blanco where the squadron had anchored at nearby St Julians on February 18 of the previous year. From there it was a hazardous journey 1500 miles north to the Rio Grande by Bulkeley's dead reckoning, which had to date proved more accurate than the navigation of Nutt of the Centurion. They were averaging about 75 miles a day and practically surviving on rotting raw seal meat. The men were in a continuous state of misery and mutiny. Certain people were considered as 'idlers' and allowed half rations while the word of the sovereign 'people' became the law of the boat. Bulkeley was forced on occasions to read out the riot act for the protection of the majority. But there was often open defiance of the command of this amazing gunner.

Late in December the last of the flour ration was consumed 'so that', said John Young, 'we had nothing henceforth to subsist on, but Seal we brought from Port Desire'. They continued to catch sufficient seal which a good deal of the time they ate in a putrefied state. When they finally were driven by weather close to shore Isaac Morris and seven men dived in to swim to the beach to obtain food and water, but a storm arose while the men were still ashore and blew the boat far out to sea. Bulkeley did not waste sentiment on his former shipwrecked mates. He dumped a number of casks which contained provisions into the ocean hoping the wind and waves would take them to the beach. Then he made off on the long journey towards the Rio Grande. He stated in his journal 'we hope to see them again, but at present we leave 'em to the care of Providence and the wide World.'

On January 28, 1743 the Speedwell miraculously arrived at the Rio Grande with 30 survivors. Thomas Maclean, the 82-year old cook, died of starvation within 15 miles of safety having lasted through the most arduous part of the voyage. The survivors were treated with magnificent courtesy by the Portuguese governor and his officials and passage was eventually provided back to England.

Isaac Morris and his small band who were left behind when they swam ashore were taken prisoners by Brazilian Indians on horseback and royally treated as privileged slaves, when it became known the English were at war with the Spaniards. Eventually Morris and his men were returned to Buenos Aires for a ransom of $90 per head which was put up by an Englishman in Montevideo who heard of their plight. They were then unexpectedly made prisoners on Pizarro's vessel the

Asia and survived an Indian uprising which was unsuccessful aboard ship. Finally in 1746, after spending a year in chains in Spanish prisons, three survivors of Morris' party were repatriated to England through Portugal.

Cheap, Hamilton, Byron and Campbell made an unsuccessful attempt in a small boat to leave Wager Island after Bulkeley departed but were forced to return, starved and demoralised. Local Indians then undertook to take the four men by canoe to Chiloe in a kind of shuttle service, the rigors of which almost killed them all. They wore flimsy clothes in the bitter cold and slept uncovered on the frozen ground. For food they were given scraps of uncooked seal meat. At Chiloe a more kindly tribe of Indians took pity on the starving half-frozen men and nursed them back to health. It was here the Spanish made them prisoners and transported the sailors to Valparaiso. Anson's courteous treatment of his Spanish captives and their subsequent release had a good deal to do with the frequent kindnesses the men received from the Spanish authorities in Chile.

The Englishmen enjoyed a good deal of personal freedom. The amorous adventures of Byron among the Spanish women, for whom he evidently had considerable attraction, would have done his grandson poet Lord Byron proud. By 1746 all four men had succeeded in arriving safely back in London on either Spanish or French ships. Byron later published a well known account of the adventures of his party.

In England a court martial was held to fix blame for the loss of the Wager. The Lords of the Admiralty ruthlessly sought their pound of flesh, but all the accused were acquitted and only Bulkeley was reprimanded. Few people could in several lifetimes have lived out the tumultuous adventures of Bulkeley, Young, Byron, Morris and the others who eventually returned home. The behaviour of these men had been in keeping with the tradition of daring and courage of their shipmates.

The mutiny at Wager Island, depicting Cheap shooting Midshipman Cozens

CHAPTER EIGHT: JUAN FERNANDEZ

On June 10 the Centurion was coasting along the shore of Juan Fernandez searching for a bay in which to anchor. The sight of verdure and trees with the cascading falls of fresh water that dropped into the sea was a delightful prospect to the weary mariners. Here there would be hope of recovery for the sick, though four more died that day. As they sailed in the lee of the island where the anchorage lay they looked for other ships of the squadron, but there was no sign of them. The island was deserted and quiet except for the occasional cries of animals and the screeching of brilliantly plumed birds.

Since there were three bays in all and night was falling rapidly Anson decided to wait and send in a boat in the morning to discover the best anchorage.

June 11th 1741. Anchored at Juan Hernandez Bay. Easternmost point East South West. Westernmost point West by North and the middle of the bay South South West; the ship two miles off the watering place

Fresh gales with a great sea from the eastward. In the morning it grew more and more moderate and at 8 AM. began to heave the anchor up in order to run into the proper bay, and with much difficulty and many surges at last started him off the ground and eased the ship in shore, but were not strong enough to heave the cable in above 5 or 6 fathoms. In this manner we could coast along shore and being abreast the point which forms the eastern part of the bay luffed her close in with the headway she had got and let run the anchor in 54 fathoms, the wind blowing out of the bay, and veered a whole cable. Soon after a sail appeared which drawing near proved to be the Tryall sloop. 3 seamen deceased.

When Saumarez saw the Tryall approach the island there was a deep feeling of relief combined with thankfulness that another ship had made the rendezvous. But the slowness and caution with which she entered the bay indicated that there were few men available to man her, and her condition could not be much different from that of the Centurion. Under jury rig with a handful of weary seamen standing on deck the pitiful state of the sloop was self evident. She would need whatever assistance could be given.

June 12th 1741. Anchored at Juan Fernandez
Little winds and fair. 2 PM. H.M. sloop Tryall anchored here having buried a great number of his men and most of the rest sick. At 8 PM. carried hawsers out on board the Tryall sloop which lay within us in order to heave ahead and lay the small bower for the shore anchor. Squalls were coming off the shore. Obliged to let go our anchor to secure the ship. In the morning found that our anchors were close to each other but were obliged to let him alone being employed in sending materials ashore to raise tents for the sick who now died a pace. It being impossible to conceive the stench and filthiness which men lay in or the condition that the ship was in between decks. AM. got the long boat out. A soldier died.

At night an inshore current forced the Centurion towards the beach where a sweet, warm smell of tropical vegetation wafted over the water. The evenings were quiet and balmy, the stillness broken by the groans of the sick and the howling of wild dogs. When Second Lieutenant Denis of the Centurion went ashore in the cutter to find the most suitable anchorage he brought back bales of green grass, seal meat and the hind quarters of a dog. The men feasted on the green grass, preferring it to meat.

The sick were soon transported ashore to the quickly constructed tents where they were to convalesce. Everyone from the Commodore down to the boys of 13 helped. It took over a month, with an increasing number of men at work, to fumigate and scrub clean the men's quarters. The ship was gradually aired of the overwhelming stench of disease and death.

When the Tryall entered Cumberland Bay on Juan Fernandez she was in a grotesque condition. Many unburied corpses still lay water-logged on deck when Saumarez went aboard. Like the Centurion the Tryall looked more like a wreck than a fighting ship of His Majesty's Navy.

On June 21 two midshipmen sighted from a hilltop a vessel attempting to beat into the island against contrary currents and wind. She was still some distance off and could not be positively identified. A thick haze suddenly descended and the ship was lost to sight. Less than a week later the same ship reappeared, this time trying to sail in from a different direction. She was then identified as the Gloucester. Her slowness in manoeuvring suggested that she was in severe difficulties. When she was close enough Lieutenant Saumarez was sent out in the cutter with fresh food.

June 27th 1741. Juan Fernandez
These 24 hours tolerable good weather. At 1 PM. the ship drawing near discerned her to be the Gloucester on

which the boat was sent loaded with refreshments to their assistance. She came within 3 miles of the Bay but the winds and currents being against her prevented her coming in. I went in the boat aboard her and found her in a most deplorable condition, nearly two-thirds of her men being dead but very few of the rest able to perform their duty.

The dead on the Gloucester lay everywhere. Those who could walk or crawl did so with a most excruciating pain in their joints caused by the scurvy. Captain Mitchell and the men who still remained alive barely held on to life. Rats infested the ship, gnawing away at the dead and eating the fingers and toes of the sick who were too weak to defend themselves. A pestilence plagued the ship.

July 3rd 1741. Juan Fernandez
Employed in filling our water and stowing our hold. At 7 PM. the Gloucester fetched in within two miles of the anchorage place and fired two guns which we answered and sent her our boat with refreshments. We were in hopes she might have got in but the winds baffling her she drove out again.

The Gloucester was swept out to sea for a second time on July 19 and was driven over a hundred miles away to the island of Masafuera to the westward. It was not before July 25, almost a month after first sighting Juan Fernandez and in spite of all assistance given by the Centurion, that the derelict Gloucester was finally able to anchor safely in Cumberland Bay.

From the moment the first tents, forges and bakeries were set up on shore and the sick began to recover, the encampment became a centre of bustling activity. Carpenters, blacksmiths and bakers worked industriously Juan Fernandez in surroundings of tropical beauty. Lookouts were posted on the highest hills of the island to scan the horizon for any signs of a sail, foreign or friendly. The Commodore still rightly felt that Spanish men-of-war were searching for his squadron. Also, he had not given up hope of seeing again his own missing ships. Lieutenant Saunders was sent to Masafuera in the cutter to see whether any other member of the squadron had sought refuge there. But within a few days he returned without success. Meanwhile, the sick grew better. Few men died once they were ashore. There were no flies, gnats or mosquitoes to bother them. It was an island of unique beauty.

Some traces of the life led by the Scotsman Alexander Selkirk in 1704 to 1709 still remained. He was put ashore from his ship after a dispute with his English captain. Selkirk was immortalised as Robinson Crusoe by Daniel Defoe. He had lived on Juan Fernandez in health and solitary happiness for five years before returning home.

August 17th 1741. Anchored at Juan Fernandez
At 1 PM. saw a sail in the northern quarter, on which we fired one gun to assemble our people who repaired on board. At 3 discovered her to be the store ship belonging to the squadron. At 5 PM. she anchored within us. They had been drove they told us, by the extremity of the weather very near the shore where they accidentally discovered a commodious harbour formed by a number of small islands with the Continent, laying in lat. 45° 15' South, and by this means escaped shipwreck. This place afforded them plenty of refreshment but was destitute of inhabitants; they took

one Indian with his wife in a small canoe who was come thither to wait for the fishing season and who made his escape from them, but not understanding him, they could learn no particulars.

The appearance of the Anna was like the answer to a prayer. She required no assistance and rode easily into the bay and dropped anchor. By an odd coincidence the place where the Anna had found refuge was very close to Wager Island; the survivors from the Wager who returned to England remarked that at evening they had heard the signal of the Anna's cannon. But neither knew of the other's presence until the voyage was over. The little bay where the Anna found haven is still called Bahia Anna Pink. The harbour has been named Port Refuge.

Master Gerrard of the Anna related an incredible tale. Squalls were driving his ship towards the ragged cliffs on the shore of Patagonia, when a narrow opening appeared in the wall of rock. Gerrard had cut the Anna's warps and sailed through and entered a snug anchorage where the crew had lived in relative comfort for three months until the weather moderated. There had been plenty of vegetables and sea food to cure the little scurvy which they had contracted. In July they set sail again for Juan Fernandez to rejoin the squadron. However the Anna's hull was in a terrible state. If the finding of refuge at Anna Pink Bay had been miraculous, her survival as a ship was equally astonishing. Upon examination many of her beams were shown to be broken and decayed as were all the timbers; the hull was almost totally rotten. The vessel was judged 'unserviceable and not fit to proceede on the voyage'. It was a wonder she had come this far.

The pink was stripped and her serviceable parts transferred to the Tryall. Anson paid Mr Gerrard £300 for the ship, formally thanked him for his fine services and spread his healthy crew of twelve among the other three vessels.

During this period of relative relaxation at Juan Fernandez, Saumarez had the time to make observations about the island.

This island lays in the latitude of 33° 35' south or 40 mins. south as I found by repeated observation and 85° 26' west longitude from the meridian of London calculated by continuance of my longitude from my first setting out to the different parallels of latitude and corrected by a celestial observation at the island of St Katharin's on the coast of Brasil. The distance from the Continent of Chile (by a medium in my different runs which were interrupted by currents to which these seas are subject) about 105 leagues west. On the first appearance strangers would naturally conclude it to be a barren inhospitable island affording a prospect of broken inaccessible mountains and rocky precipices, but on nearer approach are easily reconciled to it when surprised with the discovery of trees and verdure with which it is clothed, with several streams of water discharging themselves from below into the seas and forming agreeable cascades in their falls. On a survey which we took of the island we found the South East side to extend 6 leagues and the South West about 3 and the northern side 4, and nearest resembles that triangle called by mathematicians the scalinium from the inequality of the sides. Nearer the southeast point there is a small island called Goat Island but two miles off and near the east point there is a rock like a pyramid called Monkey Key. The southern part of it is flat and barren and being extremely dry and stony and entirely destitute of trees we flattered ourselves to have found on this part great quantities of goats. From the tradition of former voyages there are opinions which prevailed that the declivity of the mountains prevented a communication between the northern and southern sides. We found the face of things much altered. The place is covered with dogs of an enormous size resembling the grey hounds. These with the advantage of level surface have effectually destroyed the goats on this side, whose refuge consists of steep rocks and precipices, and probably in time will destroy them on the other, the dogs likewise having contracted an agility and swiftness almost equal to the goats. This side is seldom frequented by ships being mostly environed with steep cliffs against which a large southern swell is continually breaking, nor would be any ways serviceable from its laying exposed to a southerly wind which in the winter solstice generally presides and blows very hard. The general anchoring place is on the north side which affords three bays each of which is well provided with rivulets of water and fish but the middle bay is the largest and deepest laying open to a North East wind, about a mile in width and half a mile deep, which all ships prefer. It may be distinguished from the rest at sea by a tableland which is the highest mountain in the island, which for sailing in with appears to be a steep precipice the top of which inclines a little to the westward. Notwithstanding I call it tableland, it is far from being so smooth or level as hills distinguished by the name are understood to be. We mistook the bay expecting to see some other level surface as we ranged along the northern side yet in respect to the other mountains who are all broken precipices, it may be termed a tableland. What adds to the description is a steep peak on each end of it at some distance and much lower. This tableland bore from us at an anchor South South West. The other two bays scarcely deserve the name and may properly be called landing places where boats may find the conveniency of putting their casks on shore.

As to what regards the refreshments it seems providentially calculated for the relief of distressed adventurers who find such vegetables as are particularly adapted for curing the distempers contracted on long voyages and bad diets, especially those of the scorbutick kind; it abounding in great quantity's of water and wood cresses, excellent wild sorrell, a great profusion of turnips, the tops which we generally preferred to the roots, with great quantities of clover and oats for which I may add the cabbage tree. This latter was scarce and generally attained with great difficulty and hazzards. Goats we sometimes regaled with but found it very laborious and fatiguing to get any, the dogs being grown so numerous that they have almost unfortunately destroyed them and obliged the remainder to refuge on top of the most dangerous precipices. By continual application we were perfectly acquainted with the retreats and always observed that they went in herds each consisting of 16 or 20 goats and never intermixed with each other; and we can exactly tell by their diminishing proportionally to the numbers we shot. We were grown so expert as to be able to compute the number which might amount to 150 or 160 on the island, and scarce more as we were certain there were none on the south side. Their flesh was excellent and ate like venison. Some of the ears we observed were slit in this manner — the creatures are marked when bred up tame and perhaps might be the remains of Selkirk's nursery — all those thus distinguished being extremely old. We likewise found great relief from our feeding on fish which this bay is plentiful stored with in great variety. There are cod of prodigious size, cavallys, groupers, large breams, silver fishes, congers, albacores with many others, and a black fish somewhat resembling a carp called by our predecessors a chimney sweeper, with great quantities of dog fish of a voracious kind which often interrupted our fishing, it being observable that no fish would approach the baits while they were near to these, and I may also add sharks of an enormous largeness which often accompanied our boats and seemed exceedingly ravenous. The craw fish was likewise found in the greatest plenty conceivable and beyond any like I ever saw in largeness or goodness. We generally caught close to the sea side, often striking them with our boat hooks. Nor were the sea lion and seals excluded from our table. Through satiety or wantoness or depraved appetites we found them excellent food. The former bearing some affinity with beef and the latter not to be distinguished from mutton. We saw here but very few birds, chiefly consisting of blackbirds, hawks, owls, hummingbirds, and the pardella which burrows in the earth and mentioned by former voyagers. We saw not but the holes we frequently fell into. Probably the dogs had destroyed them all as they had likewise the cats which were almost exterminated, but rabbits were very troublesome and infested our tents nightly. The island is entirely overspread with woods on the north amongst which are several aromatic trees such as the vintners bark tree, arber magillaneus, called by some the pimento tree. A large tree resembling our ash whose leaves and bush have the property of the rue and used by us as bitters. The berries were like the dwarf lemon with tufted blossoms like the primrose, of a yellowish colour. The myrtle tree, these were the largest on the whole place, supplies us with timbers for several uses but none would work beyond 40 feet in length. It bore an excrescence like moss, growing on a small stock on the bark of the tree whose taste and smell resembled garlic, as was used by us as such. The tree excreted likewise the polipody which we found a good laxative. The cabbage I have already mentioned to which I may add the tree resembling the palm tree. Probably physical herbs might likewise abound in great plenty for besides the polipody we discovered the ash coloured ground liver wart recommended as useful against the venom of mad dogs. This grew nearer the banks and the rivulets on the flat stones. Also several kinds of maiden hair with great abundance of very high leaves with which the valleys are entirely covered and grow to an extraordinary largeness. We found a small shrub somewhat like the tilibri cherry bark tree whose bark we used as an astringent with great success as well as the pelliberry which we discovered in great quantities and is looked on as a nitrous diuretic, but as botanism is out of my province numbers of others have doubtless escaped my notice. It is highly probable that mines might be discovered here, that nitre abounds in most places and copper we extracted, besides which there are several hills of a peculiar sort of red earth whose brightness equal vermillion and with a proper management might furnish the composition for the potters of an extraordinary kind. I cannot omit mentioning the sea lions which seem as extraordinary a production as any in the creation and might justly deserve the observation of an expert naturalist. This surprising creature partakes of a double nature being truly amphibious, and divides its time equally between the land and sea retiring to the shore in the winter solstice as if actuated by innate impulse which prompted him to abandon an element which would soon grow boisterous. In the interval they engender and bring forth their young which at birth are as big as a seal full grown, and generally have two which they breed up with great care suckling them with their milk til contracted through the first stage of infancy, at which period the parents relinquish their charge and retire to the sea leaving their off spring behind which in a few months copulate living in this interim in the fresh water streams and eating such grass and verdure as grow near the banks of them. When arrived to their full growth they are from 12 to 18 feet long and 9 or 10 in circumference, and better to convey an idea of them is to resemble them to an overgrown seal though in some particulars there is a palpable difference; especially in the males who have a long bulbous substance growing on the top of their head and hangs down three or four inches below their noses somewhat like a comb which gives them a certain majestic masculine air. This the females are deprived of who have a much softer and effeminate look and are likewise of a smaller size.

The squadron now consisted of the Centurion, Gloucester and

the Tryall. Reluctantly it was accepted that the Pearle, Severn and Wager were lost. The Gloucester and Tryall were in doubtful condition but still capable of sailing and fighting. The Centurion, although serviceable, needed a complete overhaul. At Juan Fernandez she was scrubbed and her copper sheathing tightened, her planking re-caulked and wherever possible re-rigged with new rope taken from the other ships.

Juan Fernandez brought other changes, mainly in the attitude of the surviving men. The island had revived them, physically and mentally. Anson and his officers were no longer thinking of survival, but of taking the offensive as soon as possible. They had, they thought, overcome the worst part of the voyage. They knew that Spanish plunder was nearby and their yearning for fresh food was replaced by the longing for gold. If anyone had asked how three unseaworthy English ships with more than two thirds of their crew dead were to harass and plunder the coasts of Spanish America, the logical answer would have been to consider the mission suicidal. There were only seventeen marines left under old Colonel Cracherode, who seemed incapable of dying. The field guns and small arms aboard the Wager were lost. But the squadron still had sufficient fire power to be a threat to any foe.

September 8th 1741. Anchored at Juan Fernandez
Our long boat completing watering of us, at 11 AM. discovered a sail in the north east quarter at which we fired a gun to assemble our men. We observed her courses just above the horizon and began to conceive hopes she might be one of our squadron, till finding she continued her course to the eastward without hauling in for the island, we concluded her a Spanish ship, the time of their navigation drawing near.

September 9th 1741. The body of Juan Fernandez was 8 leagues distance; Goat Island WSW 11 leagues

Little winds with calms. Our men being come on board bent the mainsail, main topmast and set our rigging up and at 4 PM. were got under sail having stripped the small bower cable and made sail after the chase, which bore EBS. Got the topgallant masts and yards up; but were all night becalmed under the island. Were impatient till day light of seeing the chase who probably were likewise becalmed, but in the morning had no sight of her, though it was very clear. Mustered our men at the quarters and found 223, officers included; some of our men not being perfectly recovered and others employed ashore in different matters. Had men from the Gloucester and 5 out of the Tryall to such an extreme weakness our sickness had reduced us, having lost near 280 men since our leaving England.

September 12th 1741. Juan Fernandez 31 leagues. Lat 35° 04' S, Lon 84° 55' W

Blew fresh gales with stinging rain and cold air. At 3 AM. the wind veering to the West South West tacked and stood to the North West quarter. At daybreak discovered a sail over our weather bow on which we crowded all our sails after her. She bore down directly on us and hoisted a Spanish ensign and fired one gun on which we concluded her to be a Spanish man-of-war probably belonging to Pizarro's squadron from Conception or Batavia which made us throw overboard some provisions and some stores between decks. She mistook us for one of their consorts but being come within three or four miles of us and not having the signal returned, and as they told us afterwards finding the ship much larger than they had first imagined, they hauled close on wind and stood to the eastward, on which we tacked and crowded after her. Soon after a squall of rain succeeding obscured her for near half an hour, but clearing up found we had both weathered and foreached considerably on her. Being in 7 ½ miles we fired one of our 9 pounders and hoisted our colours, but the guns did not reach. Soon after we fired 5 of our waist guns which we discerned flew over her; having now got her within gun shot we made no doubt of soon being masters of her and got ready 4 more which we designed her very soon.

By Commodore George Anson Esq.
Commander in Chief of his Majesties
Ships designed on a particular Expedition
You are hereby Directed & required to Command the Spanish Prize Nuestra Carmila and keep as near me as possible and at any time when you find yourself at too great a distance from me you are to fire a Musquet & in case of Sepperation by any unavoidable accident you are to make the best of your way to the Island of Juan Fernandes where you are to Join me. You are also to take a particular care that no Chest nor Bale is broke open on board Her Prize and Acquaint the Seamen that if any of them are found guilty of the least imbezlement it shall forfit there share of the Prize Given under my hand on Board the Centurion at Sea this 12th September 1741.

G. Anson

September 13th 1741.
In moderate weather at ½ past noon having brought 4 of our guns to bear on her we fired them. The shot

whistling between the rigging as they informed us, made them strike the sails and bear down to us on which we hoisted our boat out and the Commander sent me on board. On my coming on board I found them exceedingly submissive and under great apprehension of ill treatment from us, but having satisfied them in that particular, I sent them on board our ships which they compiled with, with much reluctance, particularly the passengers who were terribly frightened and were 27 in number. This ship was called Nuestra Señora del Monte Carmelo, commanded by Don Emanuell de Lamora, having been 27 days from Lima bound for Valparaiso laden with sugar principally, with several hundred bales of blue cloth from Quita, something resembling our coarse broad cloth, but several of a coarser sort of different colours called by them Dania de Tierra like our obays. They had likewise some cotton and some tobacco, but this was strong and unpalatable. But what to us was chiefly valuable was 22 seroons of plate dollars each weighing 200 ½ lbs avoir dupois with 53 lbs weight of wrought silver; [with several trunks belonging to the passengers which after being searched were returned to them] their ship's company consisting of 54 whites and blacks. The ship was 450 tons and 20 years old but in this climate they esteemed it not a great age, but her sails which were cotton were very indifferent as was likewise her rigging. They had but three 4 pounders scarce supported by their carriages and equally serviceable, and no small arms of any sort. They had sailed from Lima with two more, all bound for the same place and that ship we saw at Juan Fernandez was of its number, but this was the richest of the three and we computed she amounted to besides her cargo about £17,867 which might be worth as much more brought to a proper market.

Saumarez spoke fluent Spanish and French and treated the prisoners with gallantry and extreme courtesy. The Spaniards had been used to the conduct of rough British privateers, whose exploits were embellished by the tales of the Spanish priests, who considered all non-Catholics heretics. The enemies of the Spaniards when captured were often treated with harsh brutality and they expected similar behaviour in return. But they were unprepared for the gentle manners of the British naval officers. Saumarez 'with great courtesy assured them that they would find a generous enemy in the Commodore, who was not less remarkable for his lenity than for his resolution and courage'.

The first prize to be taken was henceforth known as the Carmila Prize. The news that was obtained from de Lamorra was in many ways as important as the plunder: Pizarro had failed to round the Horn. This was a piece of welcome intelligence and Anson could now plan with greater freedom of action. The Viceroy at Lima had also assumed that Anson had perished and Spanish trading ships were continuing to travel the coast freely, not suspecting the presence of the English. De Lamorra told of the Spanish patrol that had waited to waylay the squadron at Juan Fernandez should they arrive and had departed just before the arrival of the Centurion. The Spanish soldiers who had lain in wait were ordered to 'board at once, sword in hand, which if well executed in their weak condition, they must infallibly be taken. No one was to be spared, but all were to be put to the sword without distinction.' The Spanish soldiers had surmised that the British were all shipwrecked.

Anson dined with de Lamorra, obtaining information which changed the objectives of the expedition. Lord Cathcart was dead, and had failed to close the Isthmus of Panama and thus shut off the passage of Spanish gold from Peru. Also Cartagena in Colombia had not been taken and the campaign ended in disaster with calamitous losses from fever. The grand design of their Lordships at the Admiralty to have Anson and Cathcart link hands across Panama had failed. The Commodore and his small band were now alone. At a meeting of all officers in mid September aboard the flagship it was decided that the remaining men and ships of the squadron would attack the port of Payta in Peru, Acapulco in Mexico and then go west to harry the Spaniards in the Philippines and return home by way of China. However, one thought was still dominant in the minds of men and officers alike: the capture of the great Spanish treasure ship that sailed between Manila and Acapulco. All the hardships of the voyage would be worthwhile if this could be accomplished.

Saumarez with 13 Englishmen and the black slaves of the Spaniards brought the Carmila back to Cumberland Bay at Juan Fernandez. He was told by one of his coloured crew that the Spaniards had hidden more silver deep in the bales of cloth, but he was unsuccessful in finding any more treasure. The healthy Spanish prisoners were pressed into service on the British ships, not the slightest perturbed at the thought of serving their former enemies. The Spanish were incredulous that boats as small as the Tryall and the Anna had gone around the Horn when the ships of Pizarro's squadron had failed. They could not know that the success of the English passage was due more to a triumph of will than to the strength of the ships.

To make her more effective the Anna's guns were added to the Carmila's armament. The Tryall sloop was ordered to intercept all the Spanish trade ships that plied the coast, though with the disappearance of the Carmelo it was now likely that an embargo would be placed on all shipping in the area.

Saumarez was to sail in the Carmila from Juan Fernandez towards Payta in company with the Centurion.

September 20th 1741. Juan Fernandez the westernmost part of the island South West 5 leagues
Employed the men in filling all our water casks and getting some fire wood on board. At 6 PM. the land wind receding weighed anchor and by the assistance of the Gloucester's boats towed out; this ship not being fully completed was left behind for a few days having directions to sink the pink which was cleared of all her things; she afterward having orders to proceed to Payta and keep there till joined by us (laying in the latitude of 5° 17' S). At 9 PM. being clear of the bay brought to and stowed my anchors and then made sail to the North by West. At 1 AM. fired a gun to let the Commander know of my looking for him but received no answer. 6 AM. saw the Commander laying to in the North of us, at 8 joined him. We both made sail to the westward, exchanging three of our negroes I had on board for 3 of our seamen, having now on board 12 foremast men, 4 negroes, 2 Indian boys, and 3 petty officers with 11 guns and 2 swivel mounted, besides small arms. That excepting a ship of war I should have been an overmatch for the small ships.

September 24th 1741. Juan Fernandez 87 leagues. Lat 33° 33' S, Lon 80° 13' W

Fresh gales then moderate. 6 PM. the Commander made the signal to speak with me giving me directions to stand off whenever he chased to prevent the suspicion of us being cruisers. At 12 PM. we brought to judging ourselves near the land. 5 AM. made sail to the eastward with the Commander. Found by my observation this day a strong southern current.

September 25th 1741. Juan Fernandez 96 leagues. Lat 33° 09' S, Lon 79° 44' W

The middle and latter part fresh gales with great hollow seas. 5 PM. the Commander made the signal seeing two sails, on which I stood off. He crowded after them to the southward. At seven being dark and out of sight of him tacked and stood after him. At ½ past 8 joined him and found them all three laying to. The two sails being the Tryall sloop who had taken a large merchant ship bound to Valparaiso from Lima called the Arranzazu loaded with much the same commodities as ours but not so considerable in money. The sloop had lost her main topmast and sprung her main mast. At 8 AM. made sail for the westward. At 9 the Commander bore down to the sloop who had made the signal of distress, her foremast being sprung.

The Santa Maria de Arranzazu was the largest merchantman on the coast. She was heavily laden with bale goods and sugar, a cargo that was important but of little commercial exchange value to the English in hostile waters. But she did have beautifully wrought silver objects, of Virgin Marys and saints, as well as gold which amounted to £5000 sterling. The English, showing no respect for these beautiful religious ornaments, hammered them down to fit into their treasure chests. It was surprising that the Tryall, taking water constantly, with a sprung mainmast and still under jury rig, had been able to overtake a good-sailing ship like the Arranzazu. But in taking the prize the Tryall had expended her last strength. Her timbers were badly strained, her seams incapable of being re-caulked and her rigging had failed. She would be in danger of foundering in any kind of bad weather, let alone being able to chase further Spanish prizes.

Saunders of the Tryall came on board the Centurion and presented a written petition signed by all her officers. The Tryall was in worse condition than anyone had suspected. For two whole days the pumps had been manned constantly to keep her afloat. Some of her seams had opened to six inches and without sail to steady her she plunged heavily in the Pacific swells. There were no materials for repairs available and if there had been, repairs could not be carried out. Anson ordered Saunders to put all stores and guns aboard her prize and to scuttle the ship without delay.

September 27th 1741. Juan Fernandez 100 leagues. Lat 32° 33' S, Lon 79° 33' W
Fresh gales with little wind. At 5 PM. went on board the Commander as per signal and received orders to cruise with Captain Saunders off Valparaiso keeping the high land of it North North West 12 leagues to intercept all ships coming out of that port bound to leeward, the Commander intending to cruise to windward of it to wait for those going in. At 11 PM. parted with the Commander who stood to the southward. At 6 PM. sent my boat to assist the Tryall in removing her stores on

board her prize, the Commander having ordered her to be sunk, the springing of her masts and proving leaky having rendered her unserviceable; were all three laying to the Eastward.

The size of Anson's fleet was unknown to the Spaniards. All the stories of terror, quite unjustified, that preceded the activities of the squadron grew on their own account. No one knew where Anson would strike next. Indeed, the very fact that the English ships existed when they were supposed to have perished surrounded the small force with the myth of invincibility. In a way the enemy was defeated before it was attacked.

In early October the Carmila and the Centurion sailed together to rendezvous with the Gloucester cruising off the coast of Valparaiso. The Tryall was scuttled on October 4. From here they would go further north to the Peruvian town of Payta which held out the prospect of loot. It was an easy sail northwards. After three days they sighted a Spanish ship and the Centurion, crowding on all her canvas, set out in pursuit. Late that evening the Centurion captured her. She was the Santa Teresa de Jesus bound for Callao, rich in cargo, but poor in dollars. Nevertheless, she supplied important food, cordage and wood for the squadron. The Spanish captain, Don Bartolo Urrunaga, was terrified for the safety of his wife and two daughters, but the gallant Commodore assured him that they would not be harmed. Instead of the plundering and killing that was expected Anson invited the captain to dinner and said he would prefer not to see his family for fear of unduly alarming them. Urrunaga was so overwhelmed with gratitude that he offered to guide an expedition against Payta and to assist in every possible way with the squadron's plans.

In early November, Saumarez on the Carmila caught up eventually with the Commodore off Pisco, not far from Payta. Saumarez was short of food and the Centurion transferred supplies aboard. Also, the prisoners on the prize were becoming a burden. They were a drain on the water and food supplies of the squadron, which had now been at sea for almost three months since leaving San Fernandez.

On November 10 the Nuestra Señora de Carmine was captured off the coast of Peru in a dead calm by the action of three of the small boats from the Gloucester and Centurion. An assault with cutlasses and pistols drew a quick surrender. The Carmine was a vessel of some 150 tons 'deeply laden with steel, iron, pepper, cedar-plank, snuff, rosarios, European bale goods and other species of merchandise', but with very few dollars. Unfortunately, the English could only use the material for which they had need. The cargo was worth £40,000 or more on the open market, but there were no means of selling the goods. However, the capture of the Carmine brought important intelligence. 'Her information made amends by acquainting us of a bark richly laden lying at Payta who was to sail the very next day bound for San Sonate with a very considerable sum of money to purchase part of the Manila ship's cargo at her arrival at Acapulco.'

Among the captives on the Carmine was a boisterous Irish adventurer, John Williams, who had roamed the countryside of Mexico as a pedlar and was now under forced employment as a seaman. He knew Payta intimately having spent some time there in jail. There was no doubt that the city had much treasure, but the coast of Spanish America was already alarmed at the British presence. The squadron would strike immediately at Payta and then leave forthwith for Mexico in search of the galleon.

CHAPTER NINE: THE SACKING OF PAYTA

At 10 pm on November 13, 1741, the Centurion lay off the Chilean town of Payta under a moonless sky. Payta consisted of several hundred houses, a fort and garrison. In the fort, the homes, the custom houses and churches was considerable wealth in dollars, jewels and gold. Mulattoes and black slaves added to the Spanish population of about a thousand inhabitants. From the boats the men of the Centurion and Carmelo went silently ashore, armed with pistols and cutlasses, under the command of Peircy Brett and Augustus von Keppel.

The sacking of Payta was over almost before it began. As one observer noted the people 'were more solicitous about the means of flight than resistance'. All the inhabitants and soldiers fled to the hills at the sight of the English, leaving their mulattoes and black slaves behind, who cooperated with the invaders, showing them the whereabouts of large stocks of brandy in addition to gold.

The Spanish governor was surprised in his bedroom by Brett and escaped by jumping out of the window in his nightgown, fleeing to his comrades in the hills, and leaving behind his beautiful young bride who sat up in bed, shocked at the appearance of a young English officer. Brett apologised for the intrusion and closed the door hoping the young woman would dress. A few moments later when he looked in again the governor's wife was being carried off through a rear entrance by a black slave.

The English sacked the town at will. Saumarez, as Anson's first officer, was ordered to remain aboard in command of the ships.

November 13th 1741. Anchored in Payta Road Town South East by South distance 4 miles

Fair with little winds, and standing in for shore. At 10 brought to and sent the boats armed with 50 men to surprise the town in the night time. At 12 PM. the island of Lobos bore east 6 miles. At 1 AM. made sail after our boats for the road. At 6 were abreast of Pena Oradada, or 'hole in the rock'. At 8 had the road and town open on which we discerned our flag flying at the fortification, the wind blowing directly off made it very troublesome plying in. At 11 one of our boats came off acquainting us with the surprisal of the town at 2 in the morning on which they became masters of it with only the loss of one man and one slightly wounded. On the first landing they had fired two guns at them from the fort and a few small arms from the governor's house which is adjacent to it and had all fled to the neighbouring hills where we discerned them in the morning. The bark we were apprised of was to have sailed this same morning, whereby we became masters of her treasure and might probably had much more had not a vessel arrived to alarm them by having being chased by the Gloucester some days since; on which the inhabitants removed or concealed most of their effects. This boat was laden with church plate and seroons of dollars.

November 14th 1741. Anchored in Payta Road

The Commander came to about 4 PM. abreast the town but she could not ply in til 8 in the evening when I anchored in 14 fathoms. AM. sent the boat to assist in getting on board the plunder and fresh provisions consisting of hogs, sheep, goats and fowls. Discerned several horsemen on an eminence over the town who constantly assembled there but never offered to molest us in our possession of the place. All the boats employed in carrying the money aboard the remainder part of the day. One of our prizes could not anchor til about 11 this morning.

November 15th 1741. Anchored in Payta Road

Fair weather. Employed in bringing in the monies on board the Commander and making strict search in all the houses suspecting they had concealed underground some of their treasure. This evening we enforced our men on shore observing great bodies of the enemy assembling near a cross upon the hill, but received no molestation from them this night. This morning received from the shore 9 negroes who had surrendered themselves, being slaves in hope of getting their liberty and likewise several seroons of jesuits bark; but concluded we had all the money in our possession having searched all the places where the slaves informed us it was likely they might have concealed their effects, and having got to the value of £30,236 08sh 00d sterling in gold dollars and wrought plate besides several gold bracelets and rings set with jewels whose intrinsic value we could not determine. About noon sent all the Spanish with most of the Indian prisoners ashore. In all

89 persons. Reserving all the negroes for the ship's use to assist in working of her.

November 16th 1741. Island of Lobus South East by South 9 leagues. By my account Island of Lobus lays 86° 34' W longitude from London

Little winds with hot sultry weather. Having plundered and ransacked the town, at 1 PM. the Commodore gave orders to set it on fire which was immediately executed, several barrels of pitch and tar having been deposited in different places for that purpose; but we spared the two churches in it. In an hour's time the whole town was entirely in flames and the fire raging very fiercely; having nailed the cannon in the fort our men embarked and went on board two half galleys whom they towed out and sank with two snows and a bark but carried the ship out with us having on board some small quantities of wine and brandy. This was the vessel which was designed to have out all the money which we found. At 7 PM. began to purchase our anchor but was 11 ere we were all under sail finding our anchors very deep in the mud. We then steered out to sea leaving the town all in flames. At daylight the Commodore gave orders for the squadron to spread themselves, consisting of six sails, in order to look for the Gloucester, which we immediately did but had no sight of her this day.

For three days the small British force had systematically looted Payta, in spite of the several hundred Spanish soldiers and horsemen who assembled on the hill above the town, playing martial music, but showing little inclination to meet the enemy in combat. All the wealth that could be carried was removed including usable live stock and provisions. In a mood of revelry many of the men dressed themselves in Spanish finery so that the looting at times took on a carnival atmosphere. The Commodore, impressed by many of the black men's cooperation during the attack, kept one of the Jamaican slaves as his valet. The Irishman Williams vanished in the early hours of the fight.

Saumarez's estimate was that the loot amounted to about £32,000, but this was conservative. The Spaniards calculated that they had lost over one million gold dollars. The true extent of individual looting and pillaging was never known, but was undoubtedly considerable. All the slaves who wished to serve on the squadron's ships were given their liberty and taken on as members of the crew. However, very few of them were able to survive the hardships of the voyage. When the squadron left Payta it sailed north up the Peruvian coast, and comprised five vessels of which only one was English. A few days later they met the Gloucester which had captured in the meantime two Spanish prizes with £20,000 in gold and silver.

CHAPTER TEN: EXPLORING THE MEXICAN COAST

The eight ship squadron was more formidable in appearance than in strength. The Centurion and Gloucester were the only vessels remaining out of the five original men-of-war and two store ships that began the voyage.

The coast of South America from Chile to Peru was in alarm and confusion. The Spaniards had been plundered before on sea and land by British buccaneers like Drake, Shelvocke and Dampier, but they had never been raided in such a disciplined fashion. By comparison it must have been almost a pleasure for the Spanish colonies. There was no rape, no wanton killing. The squadron had created an atmosphere of fear and panic that hardly justified its size. But what it lacked in numbers it made up for in the audacity and toughness of its crew. Acapulco lay ahead. This Mexican port was the place where the treasure ship, known as the Acapulco galleon when it went east, was loaded with its gold and silver for the yearly return journey to the Philippines. The Spanish ship was of such fabled wealth that its true value had never been accurately calculated. As Cathcart had failed in Panama Anson would use the discretion vested in him by the Admiralty and take the China route home; once around the Horn was enough. The wide Pacific was much more inviting, and if he should miss the galleon at Acapulco he would stalk it at Manila. The design of life had now been reduced to that purpose. All else was incidental to the moment when the squadron would first sight the treasure ship.

The prisoners acquired since Payta were becoming an unwanted responsibility. Twenty were sent ashore in a bark from Gloucester off the Ecuador coast with a week's supply of food and water. Meanwhile the captured Spanish vessels turned out to be such poor sailors that two of them were stripped and scuttled. After having drifted north through the suffocating heat of successive calms the squadron caught a light steady breeze early in December and finally sighted the island of Quibo off Colombia.

December 3rd 1741. Island of Quibo in latitude 07° 30' N bore north 61° 53' W, distance 7 leagues. Lat 07° 19' N, Lon 88° 04' W

At 4 PM. saw the land from the westward to the North North West 7 leagues distance. We tacked close off having apprehension of sailing in the night time, there being some shoals laid down in the entrance of the channel. At 1 AM. tacked and made the signal and stood to the northward and found one of our main topmast's back stays broke, our rigging being in general very bad likewise our sails by the continual rains we had. At 10 AM. were taken astays with a hard squall at the south at which we stood to the southward. At noon bent the topsails.

December 4th 1741. Southernmost part of Quibo West South West 6 leagues. Lat 07° 16' N

Squalls with much rain, then fair and moderate. At 3 PM. tacked and made the signal and stood to the northward. At 8 PM. the east end of the island Sebaco north by east 6 miles. At 2 AM. tacked with a signal and stood to West North West. The Gloucester not being able to weather it tacked, by which we lost company with her.

Aboard the Carmila Saumarez stood on course for Quibo so that he might find the fresh water springs where the almost empty casks could be refilled. Quibo had been used for over a century by British mariners for this purpose.

December 8th 1741. Watering Place North West ¾ mile. Eminence of the Island West ½ North
Anchored off the island of Quibo, the southernmost point in sight South East 5 miles distance. These 24 hours little winds and fair, at 1 PM. anchored in 15 fathoms muddy ground and hoisted boats out to water the ships and then returned to my post on board the Commodore. I kept the boats employed all night in watering the ships; sent the fishermen with the turtle nets who got several very large ones, and excellent. AM. heeled and scrubbed the ship, sent the Theresa's sails on board each prize with some of her cable to make ropes of.

Quibo was rich in wild life, with more deer, monkeys and iguanas about than any of the men had seen before. Thousands of giant turtles floated in the sun a few hundred feet offshore forming an island of their own. They were slaughtered by the hundreds. Without the abundance of turtle meat there would not have been enough food to sustain life. The young roasted monkeys tasted like chicken. Some deer were shot and there was a plentiful quantity of wild fowl. Fresh water cascaded out of the hills in cold, clear streams to fill the depleted casks. Trees were chopped down to wood the cauldrons. In the island's streams enormous alligators were occasionally shot for sport. From the dense jungle pumas emerged, occasionally coming down to the sandy beach to feast on the remains of the turtles left by the crew.

The course for Acapulco was plotted on the large scale, rudimentary charts of Halley. Although the squadron's sailing directions were more than seventy years old they were all they had to rely upon. Brett would be making more reliable charts as they sailed up the coast of South America to Acapulco, gathering as much data as he could from his constant sightings of the coastline and information on the Spanish draughts. By now it was apparent that some of the Spanish ships were in bad condition, particularly the Carmila. The Carmila could still be sailed but repairs were essential for any long voyage. No one knew exactly when the time would come for the remaining vessels to be abandoned. But it could not be long. On the Gloucester the pumps were manned constantly. Only the Centurion seemed to possess the vitality to fulfil her mission. After a brief stay at Quibo the squadron pushed on northwards.

Up the coast along Ecuador and Colombia, skirting the Cocos Islands off Panama, they slowly drew close to Mexico. The strong northern current helped the fleet onwards to its destination.

December 11th 1741. Southernmost part of Quibo North West West and Quicare latitude 07° 15' N bore North West by West 7 leagues

Moderate and cloudy. 4 PM. the island of Quicare bore North West by West 7 or 8 leagues. At 5 discerned sail to the northward of us which we gave chase, but night coming on lost sight of her for about one hour when we discovered her again and brought her to. Found her a small bark from Panama bound for Cherigui [called the Jesus Nazareno]. Having some oakum and few jars of brandy and about £42 in small money; we took her in tow and stood with the other ships to the southward. By letters on board her and their own accounts we learned again of the melancholy news of the ill success of our arms at Carthagene with a great mortality of sickness that attended them. 6 AM. the island Quicare bore North West 10 leagues. At 7 saw a sail to the north which we chased and found to be the Gloucester which we joined and spent the remainder of the day in clearing our barge in order to sink her.

December 12th 1741. By my account Island of Quibo in 07° 15' N, 88° 31' W from London. Island of Quibo North East by North distance 81 leagues

At half past 12 had a hard squall of wind and rain which lasted near two hours after which the weather proved moderate the remainder of the 24 hours. At 3 PM. scuttled and sunk our barge having cleared her. At 6 PM. made sail being 5 ships of us. Point Mariato bearing North East by North 9 leagues. Stood to the South West in the hopes of finding the weather more settled as likewise to get in the trade winds which blow from the North East board.

On December 26 the Cocos Islands were seen about 25 miles to the north west. Saumarez in his calculations estimated the island was placed 60 miles too far off the coast. Captured Spanish charts placed the Cocos 120 leagues off instead of 100 which was Saumarez's estimate. Set alone in the Pacific, the

Cocos was an important feature; a correct heading from the Cocos would lead the squadron directly to its destination in Mexico.

January 27th 1742. Island of Cocos 386 leagues. Lat 16° 31' N, Lon 108° 59' W
Continuing fair serene weather. This morning were in expectation of seeing land. The Gloucester made the signal of discovering it but it proved a fog bank. One of our negroes died suddenly of an apoplectick fit. Found the variation to be 20 East.

January 28th 1742. Island of Cocos 379 leagues. Lat 17° 11' N, Lon 108° 05' W
Moderate and fair; the air perfectly serene and pure with a certain freshness in it; very reviving. We were in expectations of seeing land the whole day. Tryall prize in the night time going ahead to sound. Caught many turtles this day.

January 29th 1742. Island of Cocos 374 leagues. Lat 17° 40' N, Lon 107° 28' W. Two homocks over Acapulco North by East 91 leagues
This land much northward of Acapulco as we found later.

Moderate and the latter part calm. At half past 9 PM. discerned a light on the port bow as we were standing in for the shore with the wind at north west. As it resembled a ship's light we conceived hopes it might be the Manila ship on which we cast off our tows to give chase and prepared everything for an engagement. This light flattered our expectations all night at different times appearing as within gun shot it kept us in suspense until daylight, when we discovered the land and found we had been deceived by a fire on the shore which burnt all day on a high mountain, but in the nature of a volcano. This light when we first discerned it was no doubt 20 leagues as our run by the log and the distance at daylight showed, and yet so far deceived us to keep all our hands at their quarters expecting to have engaged every hour. At sun rising the land extended from the North West to the East ½ North. The ship about 9 leagues off the shore. Two homock-like masses bore North which an Indian informed us were off the harbour of Acapulco.

The land on each side appearing very high, which he likewise told us was an infallible mark, the coast being generally low both to the east and west. He appeared confident, we doubted much of this the place being by observation in 17° 34' N which when included with the bearings made Acapulco to lay in 17° 55' whereas most books lay it in 17° and one or two Spanish manuscripts we found in 17° 20'.

January 30th 1742. What we judged to be two homocks over Acapulco North North East 14 leagues. Found ourselves afterwards mistaken. Lat 17° 12' N

In the latter part blew fresh from the North West. PM. made the Gloucester's and Tryall's signal. The Commodore having altered the signal from guns to false fires with the usual lights. At 6 PM. two homocks over Acapulco bore North by West 7 leagues. This night saw the same fire on the shore which had deceived us before and appeared to us rather as a beacon or signal to denote the harbour it being too small for clearing of ground or too steady for a volcano; stood off all night in the hope of getting 9 or 10 leagues to the westward of the harbour. 6 AM. the ship 13 leagues off.

What Saumarez had seen were the twin peaks of the burning volcano of Colima. Although two of the prisoners had said this was the entrance to Acapulco harbour they were wrong. The shore of Mexico had been reached but there was no sign of the Spanish galleon. Instead, they saw a barren, sun scorched beach stretching away as far as they could observe in either direction. When at noon a sight was finally taken it was discovered that they were definitely not near the latitude of Acapulco. But neither were they sure which way Acapulco lay. Accordingly on February 7, 1742 a boat under Lieutenant Denis, with Keppel and Scott, one Spanish prisoner and one black sailor was sent down the coast in search of the harbour and to gather intelligence.

February 7th 1742. What we judged to be the land of Acapulco East by South distance 17 or 14 leagues. A small island North West by North 7 or 8 leagues distance. Lat 18° N
Hot sultry air with little winds intermixed with calms. At 2 PM. the Commodore sent the 18 oared boat to range along the shore and if possible to discover where the harbour lay. Suspecting ourselves to the westward of it from our latitude; we finally discovered the homocks which might be the pass they mentioned but could not discern the round hill which is said to lay to the westward of it and an infallible mark to distinguish it by, but our Indian persisting in it we sent him with the boat. No voyagers have likewise mentioned a small island

which might have given us a sure token to know it by. If it proved to be the port of which the Indian seemed confident, all books and charts who have laid it down are most egregiously erroneous being between 20 and 30 leagues too southerly. This evening were about 6 leagues off the shore, it extending from the North by West to the East North East, extremely high and mountainous; kept plying on and off all night. At daylight were about 3 leagues off having gained some westing. Having plenty of turtle we served them to the people in lieu of salt meat to prevent if possible any relapses into the scurvy. We observed the critical time to catch them was chiefly between the hours of 10 in the morning and 2 in the afternoon in the heat of the day, when our boats have got 30 or 40 each. They generally weighed about 400 lbs and were excellent.

On February 13 the boat was sent with the same five men for a second time inshore to find the bay of Acapulco. All possible precautions were taken to guard against discovery. Everyone felt certain that the treasure ship awaited them in the harbour. It did not seem possible that after what they had already endured Providence would not deliver the galleon to them.

The Centurion, Gloucester and the three Spanish prizes took stations well offshore, fanning out in such a way as to cut off any possibility of the galleon's escape. Inshore, the Centurion's small boat hovered outside the harbour hidden from sight in the haze. Her instructions were to signal immediately should the galleon leave her anchorage. All during late February and March the squadron waited patiently at their stations for a glimpse of the Acapulco galleon.

Two black fishermen captured in Acapulco harbour by the small boat divulged that the treasure galleon had arrived as expected in January, three weeks before the squadron. The presence of the squadron was common knowledge. Messengers had been dispatched overland by the Viceroy in Lima to warn the garrison, which was defended by twelve hundred Spaniards and several hundred Indians, with 19 batteries. Because the squadron was late and really no longer expected, the not overly vigilant Spaniards had removed the sentries at the harbour entrance permitting the capture of the local fishing boat. As time wore on it was becoming doubtful if the galleon would sail that year. In another month the wind for a China trip would be wrong, which meant not only that the galleon could not sail but that the British would be prevented as well. The possibility of attacking the town was carefully considered and rejected as impractical. 'We began to despair of the Manila ship ever coming and reputed this to their apprehensions of our being on the coast waiting for her. They had already had intelligence of our burning Payta before we took three negroes from thence.' Time was not on the side of the squadron. The heat was unbelievably intense, the sun merciless as the men sweltered day after day on the rolling ships in the huge Pacific swells. The small boat spying nightly from the harbour's entrance saw no activity in the town and no sign that the galleon intended to depart. Not only was an attack on the town out of the question, but the element of surprise had been lost. Also the squadron's water supply was becoming dangerously low. Anson decided to wait a little longer in the hope of intercepting the galleon; and if she did not appear he would leave for Chequetan.

To Mr Philip Saumarez

Lieutenant of his Majesties Ship Centurion

When the Manila ship is discoverd the Prizes will join Captain Saunders keeping close to him, who will stand after me in the chase; when I hoist a white flag at the mizon peak the officers on board of the Prices will without a moments loss of time embarque their men and Indians and come on board of me.

When the Manila ship is discovered by the boats in shore they will stand off, and hoist on a sprit fixed to their mast head a red flag the signal for her standing to the eastward and a white flag the signal for her standing to the westward. On observing of which the ships in their stations will repeat the signal from one to another 'till answered by me, by hoisting a red flag at their main topmast head for discovering the enemy's ship standing to the eastward, and a white flag at their foretopmast head for her standing westward. The ships in their stations are to keep a very strict look out in shore, in the night for false fires from the Boats, the ship that discovers that signal will repeat the same. When the Commodore would have the Tryalls men and boats come on board of him he will hoist a red flag at the fore topmast head.

When the Commodore would have the Gloucester and Tryalls men both to come on board of him he will hoist a Spanish Ensign at the main topmast head.

March 4th 1742. Two homocks over Acapulco North North East 18 leagues distance. Lat 16° N

Made the proper dispositions for cruising after the Manilla ship laying in the harbour of Acapulco which our prisoners informed us was to sail near this time; we took as many men out of our two prizes as they could possibly spare and the Tryall prize sent 20 of her men on board the Gloucester to reinforce her, besides which they had orders to send the remainder of their hands on board of us or the Gloucester, either of which happened to be nearest the chase, after which the Tryall was to take the prizes under her care and stand after us; the Commodore likewise sent the two cutters to lay off the port at 4 leagues distance to observe when she came out and give us intelligence, who kept at 14 or 15 leagues distance, the Carmilla laying to West North West of us 3 leagues distance, the Tryall prize to the leeward of us to bear East by South 3 leagues distance. The Gloucester to bear East ½ South the same distance from the Tryall and the Carmen East ½ North and equal distance from the Gloucester and in case of seeing the boat to communicate it to each other by such flags as would denote whether she was gone east or west, and wait til the signal arrived to them. By noon our ships were all in their proper stations and we had sight of each other.

All the careful planning proved futile. The galleon didn't budge from her mooring. A conference on board the Centurion towards the middle of March made the decision to water and victual immediately in preparation for the long voyage to China. The harbour of Chequetan (also known as Seguatenejo) used by Drake in 1536 and Dampier in 1686 was chosen.

The short passage involved was typical of navigation in that period: the ships were inefficient sailers against the wind; the exact location and marks were uncertain; currents were largely unpredicted and had to be deduced; the harbour was uncharted and boats were sent in ahead.

March 24th 1742. Land of Acapulco North North East Distance 14 leagues. Lat 16° 16' N
Hazy, moderate weather. Plying on and off and expecting our boats. At 5 the land at Acapulco bore

North North East or 13 leagues, the Tryall being come up with us sent her boat on board. 6 AM. discerned from the masthead the two boats a great way to leeward of us on which we bore down to them. They had watched the harbour very strictly and had no sight of the ship coming out of which we began to despair of seeing her this season or probably at all, being under necessity of watering our ships made the signal for the Commander that we intended to visit the port of Seguatenejo, laying about 30 leagues to the windward of this place, where in the Spanish books mention is made of a rivulet of water being there; it was likewise here that Sir Francis Drake is reported to have careened and watered his ship.

March 26th 1742. The Land of Acapulco North North East East 17-18 leagues. Lat 15° 58' N
Little winds and hazy with hot sultry weather. Plying to the westward with our ships. AM. began to unload the Carmen with out boats and received several bales of European goods, several boxes of horse shoes and nails and several chests of steel and 4 chests of medicine with two large looking glasses.

While the squadron sailed for Chequetan, Lieutenant Hughes and six men were left in the small boat to watch the harbour of Acapulco. Should the galleon set sail he was to go immediately up the coast the hundred miles to Chequetan where the squadron was watering and warn them. The boat had provisions for twenty-four days. No one anticipated they would need more.

April 4th 1742. Port of Acapulco estimated distance 70 leagues. Lat 17° 17' N, Lon 108° 04' W

Moderate gales and hazy. At 3 PM. were within 5 miles of the shore. Uncertain of our watering place our boats not being returned. Several homocks bore east and west appearing like that described near Seguatenejo. At last we discerned a small white island or rock to the eastward of us lying near the shore to the westward of that homock which lays 8 leagues to the leeward of Pataplan. This our people who had coasted it in our boat remembered to have seen to leeward of Seguatenejo or Pataplan, by which we determined where we were. We likewise from the masthead discerned two of the four rocks laying to the westward of Pataplan the rest being in one with this; likewise this served to clear up our doubts that we were to the westward of the watering place.

April 5th 1742. Acapulco 60 leagues. Lat 17° 11' N, Lon 108° 37' W

These several days works are convincing proof what a strong eastern current we plyed up against having made 60 leagues distance by my account whereas it absolutely is not above 28 leagues distance from Acapulco.

April 6th 1742. Harbour of Chicatan bore North North East 7-8 leagues. Lat 17° 20' N

Moderate weather. At 3 PM. our two boats returned having found the convenient watering place 7 miles to the westward of the rocks of Seguatenejo which by the description we judged to be the harbour of Chicatan mentioned by Dampier. As we were now very short of water this was an agreeable news to us. At 8 PM. the land at Segautenejo bore North North East 7 or 8 leagues. At 6 AM. it bore North North East 7 leagues. Caught 23 turtles.

April 7th 1742. Chicatan 5 leagues. Lat 17° 25' N

The harbour of Chicatan North East bearing North 5 leagues distance. The whole part moderate hazy. At 1 PM. sent our boats to view the harbour a second time and sounding the entrance of it. At 4 PM. the harbour bore NN ½ E 2 leagues and the rocks of Seguatenejo ESE 7 miles. At 9 tacked and stood off. Our boats returning confirmed the design we had of going in; the reports of it being very safe and convenient for watering. 6 AM. the opening of the harbour NEBN 4 or 5 leagues. Made the Tryall's signal and sent her after our two prizes which were both at leeward out of sight in order to bring them in to us. Found the current setting SBW 5 fathoms.

April 8th 1742. Moored at Chicatan. Lat 17° 42' N

At ½ past noon, the sea breeze coming in stood for the harbour's mouth with the Gloucester, and at 5 PM. were at the entrance of it finding regular soundings decreasing gradually from 18 fathoms as we ran in. The ground being gravelly with stones and soft mud. At past 5 anchored with the best bower in 11 fathoms and veered and moored. The Gloucester came in soon after us and anchored without us; AM. early sent out long boats and our prizes' launches manned and armed to cover the watering places in readiness for ambushes by Spaniards or Indians; at the same time sent a party of forty men well armed into the country to attempt some discovery expecting to have found some town near us which we intended to have taken possession of in hopes of getting refreshments, as likewise to have proposed amicable terms to the Indians, our prizes having enabled us to have made them considerable presents for which things they would have brought in; at noon the Carmelo anchored here.

April 9th 1742. Moored at Chicatan
Moderate and fair the whole part, the land wind not blowing. This afternoon we filled 8 tons of water but this was very inconsiderable in regard to what we filled afterwards per day, not being provided against several inconveniences and little difficulties which we soon remedied; and then filled about 22 tons each day besides our daily expense; at 5 PM. the party who had been sent in the country returned. They had travelled about 9 or 10 miles inland in a beaten track, in which they observed by the dung of mules or horses which were still new that the place had been lately frequented. About 5 miles from the watering place they came to a cross road in which the paths divided between the mountains, one inclining to the westward, the other to the eastward; they chose the latter and probably by that mistake lost the town which in some of the Spanish manuscripts we had is mentioned to lay not far off the bay. Sometime after this they arrived from travelling in a narrow path enclosed on all sides with thick woods to a large plain or savannah; on the side of which they discerned a horseman standing as if placed as sentry and not unlikely was so, who on seeing our people clapped spurs to his

horse and rode off in great confusion dropping his pistol and hat which we took up. Our people not having presence of mind to fire at him by which we might even have wounded him or his horse and taken him, but only called to him in a friendly manner — by which he escaped and soon lost sight of them. This made them quicken their pace in hopes of reaching the town, but the heat of the day increasing and meeting with no water the people began to grow faint and fatigued and seeing no signs of habitations they returned, leaving a paper fastened to a stick on the road written in Spanish encouraging the Indians to carry on a correspondence with us promising them all as friendly treatment as they could possibly expect. But this had no effect nor did we see any of the inhabitants whilst we remained here, though probably they had their sentries on the tops of the neighbouring hill from whence they observed our motions. Next morning we reinforced our guard being generally upward of 100 men who went ashore every morning and returned at night. After this we contented ourselves with filling our water with all the expedition we could, being always on our guard without attempting any further discoveries inland.

April 10th 1742. Moored at Chicatan
Received from the Gloucester 3 casks of rice and 3 casks of flour. Got up our top gallants and set all our rigging up fore and aft. Two of our boats having been to the eastward having made some discoveries concerning the bay and watering place at Seguatenejo about 7 miles to leeward of us, found in the bottom of the said bay a large lagoon which probably in the rainy season by the

descent of the rains from the mountains may then appear like a river, but had a large bar before it on which the surf broke very high. They were going to land to have observed the situation of the place, when a party of horsemen advancing along the strand prevented them: our boats then made along shore towards them on which they halted and drew up in a line, but the boats still nearing them, they began to file off on which our men discharged their pieces which made them quicken their pace; though the distance from each other was too considerable to have done any execution; but we continuing our fire they continued into the woods; it is more than probable that had they acted with common prudence and waited til the landing of our people they might have intercepted them from their boats and perhaps taken them. Our men not exceeding 16 in both boats, the horse about 90.

During April, while the squadron provisioned at Chequetan Anson decided to scuttle the Spanish ships. The prizes were stripped of their valuable cargoes which were stored aboard the Centurion and Gloucester. Rigging, hawsers and all serviceable equipment was transferred to the last two fighting ships of the squadron. Casks of beef, pork and newly pickled turtle meat were divided between the two vessels. Even the spars, masts and sails from the Carmen were used.

However it was with considerable misgivings that Anson ordered the scuttling of the Tryall's prize. This Spanish vessel was seaworthy while the Carmine and Carmila were not, and the English officers commanding her resented becoming supernumeraries without the rights under naval regulations to any future prize money. The officers presented a petition to

Anson protesting at being made redundant. The Commodore formally replied, explaining the reason for his decision. There were hardly enough men to sail either the Centurion or the Gloucester. Anson assured the officers that no pay would be lost and they would be treated fairly. At the time he undoubtedly meant what he said, but in the English courts of law long after the voyage was over, gold took precedence over justice. In later days Anson's decision at Chequetan cast a shadow over his otherwise scrupulously fair conduct towards friend and foe alike throughout the voyage. The Tryall prize, in probably the best condition of all the ships, was thus reluctantly sunk at Chequetan and the crew divided among the two remaining men-of-war.

Meanwhile, Hughes and his men cruising in the small boat off Acapulco had not returned. By now they were ten days overdue. Stores and water on the boat were assumed depleted by this time and there was a general anxiety for their safety. Every able bodied man was needed for the long voyage to China. It was hoped they would soon appear.

The Commodore had a French cook called Louis Leger to whom he was much attached. When Leger disappeared on a lone walk through the jungle the first thought in everyone's minds was that he had deserted and decided to try his fortune with the Spaniards. After three days absence he was struck off strength. Saumarez even suggested that Leger was devoured by a stray tiger whose foot prints had been seen in the sand the day before. Not until two years later was it discovered that the cook had been captured by the Spaniards and taken to Acapulco. From there he had been transported to Spain, but escaped to Portugal. The Portuguese then sent him to England and it was thus from a French cook that the first reliable news of the squadron's activities reached home. From the amazing stories related by Leger the people felt a great surge of pride in the courage displayed by Anson's small fleet. Cathcart had failed in Panama but in the Pacific a small naval force was defeating the Spaniards at every engagement. The accounts of the voyage spread through the country so that by the time the Centurion returned the whole nation awaited her.

The finding of the harbour of Chequetan had been a welcome discovery; although it did not contain the abundance of fruits and meats of Juan Fernandez, it did have unlimited supplies of sweet water.

Saumarez surveyed the island carefully and spent several days exploring the coves and beaches, taking bearings of prominent land features and sounding the bays and the ocean along the shore line.

Description of Chicatan

About three miles to the westward of us is a small island or white rock laying near the shore. This homock and rock are seven or eight leagues to the eastward of Pataplan which is an infallible mark to discover the harbour by. This place is a peninsular of a moderate height appearing like an island ¾ mile long and joins to the Continent by a very low isthmus full of shrubs and trees. About 2 ½ miles to the westward of it is an assemblage of large rocks appearing white from the excrements of sea birds which inhabit them; there are four large ones with several little ones intermixed and by the help of the imagination make approximately the figure of a cross. About seven miles from these rocks is the harbour of Chicatan still rendered very remarkable by a large rock of a considerable height laying about a mile and a half from it. To the westward of the harbour lay likewise several misshapen rocks, but a greater distance from each other and not so compact as those to the eastward. It would be difficult to give any marks to discover the harbour if the ship is at any considerable distance from the shore; there being so many different chains of mountains behind each other which from laying double form such a variety of aspects that the alteration of one or two points entirely alters the scene and gives the land a new appearance. The entrance of the harbour is about one mile in breadth being more oval than circular, environed on all sides except the west one with high mountains overgrown with trees. Within the harbour the deepest water is 10 and 11 fathoms on the east end of it and from thence shoals apace to 6,5 and 4 ½ fathoms westward; but an allowance must be made for a large swell which at different times causes a great sea and likewise for the ebbing and flowing of the tide which rises and falls about 5 feet and sets nearby eastward and west; the watering place is on the west side of the bay and procured from a small spring bubbling up near it a quarter of a mile in the country. The assemblage of this water forms a large lagoon or canal of water which appears like standing water, having no possible discharge into the sea, between which there lays a bank of sand contiguous with the rest of the strand thro' which it imbibes and mixes with the sea and likewise when it is blown fresh and caused a great swell, it is not improbable but the sea breaks over the bank into the lagoon. We observe at different times the water is softer and fresher than it has been at other times for which reason we always filled near the spring where it was very good but the more inconvenient to come at;

but as we fell into a method of using canoes which draw little water and were loaded with barricoes we made an extraordinary discharge filling some days 26 tun. This in the wet seasons may probably appear like a river being swelled with the descent of the rains from the mountains and over flows the bank which confines it in at present, and perhaps a great part of the land near it which is low and full of mangroves. As to the neighbouring country we were almost entire strangers to it, but doubtless may afford great plenty of refreshments with the native Indians had they been communicative; however venturing far into the woods we killed abundance of pheasants, wild turkey, parrots with other birds of a small size; fruits were a refreshment we stood in great want of; finding a very few small lime bushes scattered about with some papaes of a very small kind and a sort of plum called in Jamaica the hog plum of an agreeable acid; we likewise found a herb called the brook lime growing near the fresh water side this being among the register of anti-scorbuticks. We fed very plentifully on it finding great abundance of it; we likewise found a tolerable quantity of fish particularly where the water was smooth and would prompt us to haul the tiern, being chiefly cavallys, mullets, breams, bonitos, a flat fish something like a sole and an excellent fish called the fiddle fish.

On April 28, 1742 the Centurion and Gloucester sailed out of Chequetan harbour. A note in a bottle was left in a canoe sufficiently disguised in its language should it fall into enemy hands, but quite clear to the missing Lieutenant Hughes should he find it. The weather and visibility were good. By May 4 the ships were fourteen leagues from Acapulco and being set by a strong eastern current that was taking them away from the shore. Ugly black clouds were gathering over the sea and there was an unexpressed anxiety in Saumarez's mind about the long journey that lay ahead. Instinct told him that the winds that blew were not the trades, which they must count upon to make a fast passage across the Pacific. When the two ships finally arrived within a few leagues of Acapulco the Commodore, believing the cutter and her crew were captured, sent a launch with one Spanish officer and six Spanish prisoners ashore to the governor to treat with him for the release of Hughes and his men. The officer carried a petition signed by all prisoners asking the governor to release the English and informing him of their own good treatment. The launch was to return at 6 pm the following day. On May 5 a small boat was spotted in the morning haze moving very slowly in the direction of the Centurion. Figures lay in the boat unmoving under a small awning made of sailcloth. At noon it was plainly seen to be the cutter with Hughes and his men. They were taken aboard, badly burned from the sun, weak, and half-dead from heat, but they were all still alive.

May 6th 1742. Port of Acapulco 43 leagues. Lat 14° 40' N, Lon 105° 41' W

These 24 hours found a strong, southern current, being by observation 28 min. to the southward of my accounts. Port Acapulco bore 43 leagues. First part moderate and hazy the latter fresh gales with a great head sea from the southward, ½ past noon our cutter arrived on board; they had cruised their appointed time on the station and were plying to the westward to join us but a strong eastern current setting them away prolonged the time til the water was all exhausted which obliged them to bear away to the eastward in quest of more; they coasted it along shore near 80 leagues without any possibility of finding a landing, large surf everywhere preventing them. At last a very heavy tornado in which much rain fell relieved them and filled all their casks; they had been several days before without water, and had recourse to turtles' blood which they drank in lieu; they then returned to the westward and being favoured with a strong western current in 50 hours joined us having been absent 43 days; having recovered our boat and men the Commodore put aside all thoughts of treating with the Governor. We gave all the Spaniards their liberty with most of the Indians and all the sick negroes amounting to 39 prisoners; having provided them with one of our prize's launches with masts and sails and 15 days' provisions, they intending to go for Panama; at the same time we reserved to assist us 43, chiefly negroes and mullatoes with a few Indians; the Gloucester sent away part of hers likewise in another launch. Having dispatched these boats away, at 6 PM. made sail with H.M. Ship the Gloucester, the Commander intending to leave the Coast of Mexico and South Seas and cross over to the East Indies; AM. reeved new fore topsail braces the old ones breaking.

It is unfortunate that on the day they left the Mexican coast the governor of Acapulco had sent the launch with the prisoners back to sea to meet the squadron at the appointed rendezvous. In a magnanimous gesture he filled the returning boat with the finest delicacies in Acapulco as a present for Anson. He wanted to show his appreciation for the treatment of the

Spanish prisoners. But the launch returned too late. In the far distance they could barely make out the tiny specks of the Centurion and Gloucester disappearing to the west.

CHAPTER ELEVEN: ACROSS THE PACIFIC

The Ladrone Islands lay 7000 miles to the west. Another 1500 miles further was the coast of China. Saumarez was unaware that the course he and his officers plotted was not on the route of the trade winds as he anticipated. With the progress of the seasons the trades move north while the two ships were sailing in a southerly direction. They were in fact heading into the area of the dreaded doldrums. It would be at least seven weeks before they would reach fair winds, at the end of June 1742. In the meantime, both ships were showing signs of the continual strain on both hull and rigging. The vessels were a patchwork of parts made up from the ships they had scuttled. On the Centurion and Gloucester very little was left of the original sails, spars or rigging with which they began the voyage.

May 9th 1742. Acapulco 107 leagues 1 mile. Lat 11° 35' N, Lon 106° 36' W

The whole part little winds. Grew very changeable shifting to the southward, but this we imputed to our being on the borders of the trade winds. At 4 PM. discovered our foremast to be sprung half way between the forecastle and top; the wound seemed dangerous, beginning at the after part and rounding on the starboard side near 2 inches in circumference; by which we judged it to be 4 inches thro'. This was a disagreeable sight to us who were now stretching for the East Indies and were apprehensive of arriving on the Coast on the monsoon season, which is always very tempestuous.

Having nothing on board fit to repair him, (our fishes not being thought sufficient) were supplied by the Gloucester with the Carmen's main mast 56 feet long which being Spanish elm or what they call maria wood was much stronger than fir. In the night time had several hard showers of rain.

By the middle of May the bitter certainty that they were not in the trade winds became evident. Meanwhile the carpenters worked on the mast of the Centurion in the calm weather and made it as strong as they could. The wind veered then backed. Day after day the weather was the same; calms interrupted occasionally by hard squalls, blinding rain and lightning. There was one ironic compensation: death had so reduced the crews that both ships floated high above the water. There was enough room below to breath, the ports could be opened for ample ventilation and the men slept with free space on either side. With fresh food on board, plenty of water and wood it seemed that all they had to contend with was the sea and the rotten condition of the ships.

The carpenters had strengthened the Centurion's foremast by clapping on three fishes that provided a temporary support. But the Centurion was sailing without a foresail, the canvas being so torn that the sailmakers were unable to suitably mend it until much later. On May 15 the rotten foremast was strengthened by adding on three iron hoops. Then the foreshrouds were set up and the patched sail bent. It was still far from satisfactory but the repairs would have to last until they crossed the Pacific Ocean.

On May 29 scurvy broke out among the crews and spread quickly. It was, for some unknown reason, more prevalent on the Gloucester than the Centurion. For the first time Anson himself was afflicted. A good many of the cases were recurrences in men who had suffered from the horrible illness before. Many bonitos and dolphins were speared beneath the bows but this food did little to help cure the disease. Without any sign of the trades the crew of both ships grew very dispirited. The black men were usually the first to die, and they succumbed very quickly to the scurvy. By the beginning of July there were hardly any left. But many birds were flying above the Centurion and this simple sign of life was one of the few hopeful omens about. For a few days there was wind and a brief coolness in the air.

June 16th 1742. Port of Acapulco 511 leagues. Lat 13° 34' N, Lon 131° 34' W

These 24 hours a constant settled wind at North East. We steered West North West. PM. sent one of our carpenters on board the Gloucester to repair the mast. Employed our sail makers and all who could handle a needle to mend our sails which began to be much decayed and worn. Unbent the main topsail and bent an old one; found the var. 2° 50' E.

June 17th 1742. Acapulco 448 leagues, 1 mile. Lat 13° 49' N, Lon 133° 15' W

Moderate and cloudy the whole part, the wind veering around to the north made the air extremely cool and pleasant; in the morning the wind being at North by East obliged us to steer west to favour the Gloucester carrying her steering sail. Her mast on surveying was found very rotten and decayed which obliged them instead of fishing him to cut him as low as the rotten part ran.

June 18th 1742. Port of Acapulco 568 leagues, 1 mile. Lat 13° 38' N, Lon 114° 36' W

The whole part moderate and fair, the wind continuing North by West, we steering westward. In the morning observed a great northern swell which we imputed to our being got the length of the west end of California and opening the unknown tract of land laying behind it; but were much surprised to find the eastern wind not fixed as all former voyagers in these parts have found it.

June 19th 1742. Acapulco 590 leagues. Lat 13° 28' N, Lon 135° 47' W

These 24 hours moderate and fair, the wind continuing in the northern board. This evening were surrounded by several birds called Cape Hens which made us judge there were some islands near us, the charts laying down several called the Nubilla. Set up our preventer shrouds fore and aft, the ship labouring much in a northern swell.

June 20th 1742. Acapulco 614 leagues. Lat 12° 58' N, Lon 137° 02' N

The first part and latter inclining to calms and the wind shifting to the North West by West which discouraged us much, being in suspense with thinking of the uncertainty of the wind and the distance from the land, especially when we reflected on the long run we had still to make not being above a quarter part of our passage over.

June 21st 1742. Acapulco 626 leagues. Lat 12° 40' N, Lon 137° 37' W

The first part winds and hazy, the latter calm, the wind continuing at a northern quarter with great swells from thence. AM. sent our boat aboard the Gloucester to enquire the state of the mast and found it rotten and decayed most part of the way down that they will be obliged to step the topmast on the stump of the mainmast and set the main topsail instead of a mainsail, taking the Tryall sloop's main topsail. The birds and the fish still continue about us, the latter we were industrious to get.

June 30th 1742. Acapulco 900 leagues. Lat 13° 19'N, Lon 152° 05' W

The weather moderate. A negro man and boy died of scurvy and had several more extremely ill, probably most of them will die. In the morning altered our course from the west to the south west expecting to find more wind by going a degree or two to the southward. This day caught many bonitos which was a great refreshment to our people. Variation 4° 10' E.

The winds tantalized and tormented. For a time they would blow fresh from the north east and the men believed they were in the trades and the ships finally on course. Under these conditions a hundred miles or more were covered in a day. Then a flat calm would descend and the rotten masts swayed dangerously in the hollow swells. In early July they were 4300 miles west of Acapulco. Each day Saumarez, as much weakened as any member of the crew but still miraculously free of scurvy, checked the variation of the compass which was sometimes as much as 20 degrees. What he could not have known was that the large quantities of captured iron still in the hold of the Centurion affected the instrument. But in those days there was no knowledge of deviation. Each morning and night by means of amplitudes he obtained with fair accuracy the deflection of the needle, for without the vital amplitudes they could have missed altogether the Ladrones or even the coast of Asia.

Compared with the Gloucester the Centurion was still in reasonably good shape. The Gloucester was losing as many as five men a day from scurvy. The surgeon himself had died of the disease. They had run out of all fresh foods and the fish and birds they caught lacked any quantities of the vital vitamin C that could have cured them. The limes of Chequetan contained a little vitamin, but they had been eaten in the first month.

July 1st 1742. Port of Acapulco 934 leagues. Lat 12° 15' N, Lon 153° 31' N

By this day's observation a southern current had sent me 14 minutes to the southward of my reckoning. The first part was little winds and cloudy, the middle and latter it increased and blew a fine fresh gale, yet could not improve our position much, the Gloucester being disabled; continuing our course to the south west in hopes of meeting the wind. 2 negroes died. All our people are very weak and declining. This morning we had a great quantity of birds as usual which made us conclude there might be some islands near us.

On July 24 the ship's company was mustered and it was found there were 148 people alive on the Centurion, but most of them were very sick. Seventy six had died since leaving Mexico. From that day forward the men began to succumb at a much faster rate.

The end of the Gloucester was near. She was under jury rig with a fraction of her canvas set when her rotten foremast collapsed without warning. The deck was a mass of broken spars, ropes and torn sails. Saumarez observed the chaos with a classic sense of restraint: 'these things all add to our delays and perplexes us much'. The Gloucester was a wreck, with a crew dying faster than they could be buried since there were few men strong enough to slide the dead overboard. Whoever had strength left worked the pumps trying to keep the ship afloat. Eight feet of water was in the Gloucester's hold and was slowly rising despite all efforts to pump it out. The Centurion finally took her in tow.

During the five months they had been at sea since leaving Acapulco the ships had been at the mercy of uncharted currents which reduced their dead reckoning to guesses. In spite of daily calculations from the meridian of London, their longitude was really unknown. On July 30 the top of the Centurion's mainmast broke, and it was left dangling since there was no one strong enough to climb into the upper rigging to repair it.

August 3rd 1742. Acapulco 2015 leagues. Lat 13° 19' N, Lon 209° 54' W

First part moderate and fair, the latter the wind proved unsteady attended with squalls and rain. At last it fell calm. In the evening our men returned on board having completed the rigging on the Gloucester. At 8 AM. cast her off being apprehensive of being on board each other. Observed some black birds like Cape Wrens near us with much fish. By the Spanish Manila ship's account which we have in manuscript esteem myself 42 leagues off, but our English privateers make much more to Guam. Girsham Waters seaman and a negro died.

Simon Smithers, sergeant of the marines, died on August 5. He was one of the few marines still left and by all rights should have been enjoying his last days pensioned in the English countryside playing with his grandchildren. Instead, he died from scurvy on the empty Pacific, crawling up out of the orlop on all fours and collapsing on the sun-blistered deck that had become a graveyard.

August 12th 1742. Acapulco 2135 leagues. Lat 13° 56' N, Lon 216° 11' W
The whole part it blew very hard with several violent squalls of wind and rain and a great western sea. In the middle part the gusts of wind came on very heavy, the weather looking extremely black to the West South West with lightning which made us apprehend a hurricane. At 1 PM. our main topsail splitting handed him and lay to under mainsail. In the morning we discovered the Gloucester to windward of us with her fore topmast by the board, a very disagreeable sight to all our people who grew mightily discouraged and impatient of these contrary winds which we suspect are of the westerly monsoons, and are very uncertain of how long they may obstruct our passage.

August 13th 1742. Acapulco 2133 leagues. Lat 14° 36' N, Lon 216° 05' W
Continuing blowing hard little squalls of wind and rain til 8 in the evening when the wind abated and fell calm,

the ship labouring much in a great hollow sea. At 1 AM. it came on again and blew very hard in squalls with heavy showers and thunder and lightning but towards morning it grew more moderate. 3 PM. stopped-on one of the larb'd foreshrouds which we found broke and got down the topga'tyards. In the morning unbent the main sails which had split in the night time and found another. This fatigued our people very much and we could scarce tend our pumps which grew very urgent. At noon the Gloucester being to windward fired several guns and made the signal to speak with us bearing down under our stern. John Evans and John Webber died.

August 14th 1742. Acapulco 2126 leagues. Lat 15° 03' N, Lon 216° 10' W

The first part was squally thick weather, the middle and latter it grew more moderate and cleared up. ½ past noon the Gloucester came under our stern, when Captain Mitchell acquainted the Commodore that his ship had sprung a leak and had then seven foot of water in her hold, his men with incessant pumping being all fatigued as were likewise the officers and no longer able to hold out having had 9 ½ feet of water within her; all the full water casks were entirely covered and the people had no water to drink. The ship rolled and laboured and was under no command of the helm. Soon after we hoisted the cutter out and sent her on board with the carpenter who returned in the evening. They had then recovered themselves and had gained 20 inches upon her having 5 foot 4 inches but then were no longer able to stand out; the Captain and officers having represented their circumstances with the condition of the ship the Commander sent them word he would remove them next day intending at the same time to take out what stores our ships were most in want of; it being impracticable for us to give them any assistance to preserve the ship without an apparent danger of loosing both by dividing our strength. At 6 in the morning we hoisted the cutter and pinnace out and sent our men on board the Gloucester to assist them to get the boats out and removed the people. Elias Hubert seaman died; this makes 30 since leaving the coast.

August 15th 1742. 2126 leagues from Acapulco. Lat 15° 03' N, Lon 216° 10' W

These 24 hours chiefly calm with exceeding hot sultry weather; lay to near the Gloucester under foresail and mizzen. In the evening the Gloucester's long boat came on board with 46 sick men. Most of them very ill. 3 dying in getting over the side. We received at the same time a new mainsail with some bolts of canvas. In the morning the boat brought on board a great cable, an 8 inch hawser and a messenger with some small arms and pistols. Mr Dennis Crawley boatsun departed this life, an excellent good officer, with Mr Halldane midshipman and Andrew Slaughter. Our men being very weak and much fatigued but were obliged to look hard to clear the Gloucester. In all 46 sick.

August 16th 1742. Acapulco 2153 leagues. Lat 15° 08' N, Lon 216° 35' W

These 24 hours little wind and cloudy, our people employed in clearing the Gloucester and getting on board what stores we could possibly save, that we stood most in want of. 6 PM. having got as much off as strength and time would permit us the Commander gave orders to set her on fire to prevent any possibility of her falling into the enemy's hands, as we were very uncertain what distance we might be from the land. Her people were repairing on board of us which were reduced to 97 officers and men included; 40 of which were extremely ill and confined to their hammocks, and 25 boys in all, 68 sick. At 7 she was accordingly fired having 7 ½ foot of water in her hold. We were then about 1 ½ miles from her and it falling little wind we were obliged to crowd what sail we could to get a convenient distance from her before she blew up. Our people who had been employed in firing of her returned on board the Centurion, our four or five boats towing alongside, whose crews were most of them drunk with the liquor they had rummaged on board the Gloucester. With the apprehension of a squall which threatened to take us back, the hurry of hauling down our sails which the weakness of our people rendered slow and dangerous, all this joined to the encumbrances we had on the deck of sick and dying men, the hurry and shortness of time had not permitted us to take care of and with casks and lumber received from the other ship which filled up the decks and entangled all our running ropes; these different accidents still aggravated with the prospect of the last ship of our squadron blazing within two miles of us, combined to make us as melancholy a scene as ever I observed since I have been in the navy. The remainder of the night grew tolerably moderate by which we saved all our boats excepting the Gloucester's barges which broke adrift and sunk soon after being deep laden. Our people being too much fatigued to hoist them in.

The Gloucester burned fiercely. When the flames touched the fuses of her unmanned guns they fired off one by one like lonely salutes in the night.

At 6am on August 16 the flames finally reached the powder magazines and she blew up with a tremendous explosion. A plume of black smoke shot up and the cloud spread till the wind dispersed it. Shortly after, the great rounded after cabin of the Gloucester arched into the early morning sky and descended into the Pacific.

Saumarez realised on August 18 that a northerly current was setting the ship beyond the desired latitude of the Ladrones. They were at the same time blown by a southwest wind to the north. Fortunately, before August came to an end the current reversed itself and guided the near-derelict Centurion along the latitude of the Ladrone Islands. The longitude was still unknown. Their good luck was that a current even in the dead calms carried the ship at least twenty miles a day towards her destination. Those who still had strength left were working the pumps to save the ship and themselves.

A leak in the bow had been temporarily stopped by the shipwrights but the Centurion was taking in several inches of water an hour through her open seams. It was clear to everyone that if they did not soon find a safe anchorage they would meet the same fate as the Gloucester. Or if the ship should survive there would soon be no men left to sail her.

August 23rd 1742. Acapulco 2180 leagues. Lat 16° 45' N, Lon 219° 01' W
By observation a southern current set us 5 minutes beyond our accounts.

Continuing little winds and fair blowing from the south west to the south east. At daylight discovered two islands one bearing W ½ S resembling more the appearance of a large rock than a place to anchor at but was considerable distance off. The other bore south west by west about 15 leagues distance. It appeared to be high though of an indifferent length and might be 1 ¼ leagues from the other. The sight of land spirited up our people extremely and gave us hopes we might find an anchoring place at the largest of the islands to recruit ourselves. It was the vulgar opinion amongst our people that we had sailed so far as to pass by all the land in the world. Found the variation 6° 41' E. Anthony Garganigo, Richard Wheeler, Duncan Campbell, James Brown, Benjamin Dawson seamen departed this life.

A boat was launched for the shore of the nearest island on August 25 but soon came back with the sad news that the closest island, although uninhabited, was without a suitable anchorage or watering place. But it abounded with coconuts which now filled the cutter to the gunwales. The men drank the delicious coconut milk until they were sick from it.

On August 26 there was a muster to ascertain the able-bodied in case hostile Indians or Spaniards should be met. Altogether there were 71 officers, boys and men who could still move and carry out minor duties, though many among the 71 were afflicted with scurvy. The following day the current carried the Centurion towards another island, where a swift native proa was seen leaving the shore. The great speed at which the proa skimmed over the water amazed everyone. Although as ill as other members of the crew and without having had a proper longitude for months, Saumarez calculated his position with amazing accuracy. The island they were closest to was identified as Ganis and they now sailed south searching for a safe harbour nearby. Anson hoisted Spanish colours hoping his ship might be mistaken for the Manila galleon, and shortly after the proa made a wide, cautious circle and then came towards the ship to greet her.

August 28th 1742. Anchored at Island of Tinian. Northern part North East by North distance 2 leagues. Southern South East South 5 miles. Island of Aguigan South West 3 leagues and a reef runs from the shore within which lay the southern bark East by South South 1 mile

The whole part little winds and fair; 3 PM. sent the boat ahead to sound and discover the anchoring place at which time a proa stood off to them, judging us to be the Acapulco ship for which mistake they were made our prisoners. There were about 7 men in her all unarmed, two of which were Spaniards and the others Indians. These people informed us that this island was uninhabited and was used by the Spanish garrison at Guam as the magazine on which they had their supplies of provision, it being plentifully stored with wild cattle and hogs and poultry. They were sent by the governor to kill beef which they were preparing in the sun to dry and were to load the small barge which was in the shore and then return to Guam; there being 21 of these people in all partly Spaniards and Indians. He who then gave us this intelligence was the officer being a Sergeant, a native of Guam. He likewise added that here were great quantities of limes and oranges and a certain fruit called the breadfruit, peculiar to the island resembling in flavour and size a great potato and in appearance something like a shaddock, of a middling size in the West Indies Islands; this discovery seemed as the direction of a peculiar providence, it being impossible that the ship could have continued many days more at sea, there being few people of sufficient strength or numbers to navigate her and keep her above water, our pumps fatiguing us all to death, and even those officers all on the decline were exhausted. The bark being all the embarkation that was left we sent the boat to take possession of her to prevent it returning and making the escape and at 8 P.M. anchored in 22 fathoms with the best bower; but not withstanding it was almost calm were near 5 hours in furling the sails, the manning our two boats having deprived us of all our able seamen. In the morning sent some hands ashore to raise some tents for the recovery of our sick but there being found huts sufficiently large to contain them all we proceeded to clear the ship and by noon had sent 54 sick men ashore. This island was called Tinian. That high land to the northward which at first we thought had been contiguous to it was an island called Laypan and the small one to the south west of Tinian was called Aguiga, but all uninhabited. Mitchell Merril boatsun, George Meager, Charles Boyle, Fulham Pitt, William Newman, Matthew Broadmead, Dennis O'Brien and Timothy Coughlin seamen departed this life. This makes 93 white men.

August 29th 1742. Anchored at the Island of Tinian
This morning sent our sick ashore making it in all 128. Hoisted the long boat and lay ready for the first wind to new berth the ship and run farther in this being foul

ground. Thomas Brunnel, armourer, Peter Bell a boy, John Silks a marine, Abraham MacCarthy, William Angel and Thomas Marshall seamen died. This makes 99 men. Employed til night in sending our sick men ashore and the weather promising fair, kept most of our able men to guard them in case the Spaniards had deceived us in their numbers. In the evening three more of the Indians came to us one of which was an inferior officer, who undertook to carry the people to a certain savannah or plain 9 miles off where he promised to kill cattle for us; accordingly we sent three with him who when they were arrived at the proposed place trusted him at his request with a musket and pistol with which soon after he made his escape on pretence of having to shoot an ox, our people seeing called to him but he persisted, they fired at him and missed him whereby he got off and this made us alter our treatment to those we had in our custody, especially the officer who before was used with great courtesy, suspecting he was privy to this behaviour. He strongly denied this offering to send one of the Indians to the rest of the Spaniards with orders to deliver their arms and surrender themselves and drive the cattle to us; this at last was accepted and the one was sent; in the meantime we kept those we had on board under strict confinement to wait the event of his return.

When the sick were tended the able bodied began work on the ship. All guns, shot and moveable materials were carried aft so the bow would lift from the water. Then the shipwrights cut away the rotten timber around the leaking stern which was recaulked. However, when the ship was trimmed the leak persisted. Three times in their weakened condition the men shifted cannon, shot and materials forward and aft, until finally the cause of the leak was found to be a bolt hole.

In the meantime the crew gorged themselves with beef and fruit. With long periods of rest the survivors slowly regained most of their health and stamina.

Description of the island of Tinian and other Ladrone islands
This island called Tinian by the Indians its primitive inhabitants, and Bonavista by the Spaniards lay in 14° 54' north latt. and situated 114° west from Acapulco, seems to have remained entirely undiscovered by all former voyagers who usually kept in the parallel of 13° in order to fall in with the island Guam; unless it be this place Ferdinand Magellan discovered in his passage from America his latitude having made affinity with this, where he met with a vigorous resistance from the inhabitants who were very numerous and surrounded his ships with the proas, but at present remain uninhabited, the Spaniards having compelled the Indians with those of the other islands in the year 1718 to retire to Guam and Rota which two are of the most considerable of all the Ladrone islands. This our Indian prisoners informed us and that the natives regretted this move to such a degree that in a few years they all broke their hearts with grief; this place if we may credit our Indians, once contained near 32,000 inhabitants and they showed us the ruins of the village which contained a thousand adding that the island was formerly full of such places. At present there are few remnants of any habitations, excepting several double rows of square pillars dispersed about the island and containing 8 or 10

in each rank with a kind of half globe at the top, the flat part upwards; on these we were informed were the houses erected raising them probably in this manner to prevent the vermin and insects from annoying them as likewise to render them more airy. It is beautifully diversified with plains and groves of trees most of them coconut, orange and some lime trees. At a distance it affords a delightful prospect as any cultivated island could possibly afford. It extends itself from the N.N.W. to the E.S.W. about 6 leagues in length and 7 or 8 miles in breadth, the land of a moderate height with easy, regular ascents abounding with herds of cattle amounting, by the Indians' computation, to be eight or nine thousand, and great quantities of wild hogs with many cocks and hens flying wild in the woods with some ducks, this place being used by the Governor of Guam as a magazine wherewith he supplies his garrison. Here are no running streams of fresh water but some springs which we discovered with several old wells filled up, which in digging, clearing away the rubbish afforded excellent water but would require sometime to fill a number of casks; with all these advantages the island appears naturally calculated for the refreshment of ships as in effect it is, yet it has this inconveniency of the anchorage which is not to be relied on, the ground being full of coral rocks which would infallibly damage your cables as happened to us who parted two and narrowly escaped loosing the ship on a reef which runs from the shore, and within which small vessels may lay safely. Though it is not improbable but in making diligent search one might find better ground particularly near a small sandy white bay which lay half way between the reef and the northern part, at a place the Spaniards say is probably good anchoring; not withstanding this inconveniency this is certainly the properest place for strangers to refresh themselves at, who in a long run as from the Coast of Mexico hither seldom escape being afflicted with the scurvy, and here may find the proper medicine: viz fresh meat and fruits without molestation. The island is situated in the centre of the Ladrones and may be distinguished by two neighbouring islands, of the one bearing S.S.W. from it a distance of 3 leagues called Aguigan. It is about 4 or 5 miles long, each end terminating with regular ascents like steps and higher land than Tinian; the other called Laypan lays at the N.E. and of Tinian about 5 or 6 miles off, much higher land than the other two islands and as our Indians informed us has some streams of fresh water with fruits and wild hogs but no cattle. In the straits between this and Tinian lays a reef of rocks on which a Spanish vessel was lost some time since in attempting to sail there. This island is 8 or 9 leagues in length and was formerly inhabited; to what concerns the other islands our prisoners were ill qualified to give us any satisfactory account of them and can only depend on what we saw ourselves having an opportunity of observing 8 of them. The first we saw being called Ganis. It is near 5 miles in length and high land lays in 16° 50' N latt. 114° 18' West long, from Acapulco. It is full of coconut trees and I observed no fresh water. It has foul ground all around it. S.E. from it about 8 leagues is a small flat island called Paxosisir Ullea in the Indian dialect, abounding with birds. The island Sapana or Rota as the Spaniards call it may be discerned from Tinian bearing from thence about S.W.B.S. a distance 17 or 18 leagues; is high in the middle with the two ends appearing low and level land, and is about 10 leagues in height and may contain 400 inhabitants mostly Indians under the direction of a Spanish priest. As for the island Guam it is the principal and most considerable of the Ladrone islands having a Spanish governor and garrison but ill provided. They have a small port on the S.W. part of it which mounts 5 guns, nine posts and have 3 companies of soldiers each consisting 60 men many of them Indians. There the Acapulco ship on her passage to Manila makes a short stay taking refreshments and exchanging her sick and infirm people for others, continues her voyage; they have besides a yearly ship of 20 guns from Manila which brings them clothing and pays for the subsistence of the garrison, but this is sometimes interrupted. Our prisoners informing us there had been no ships there for these two years past which had reduced the garrison to a great inconvenience, her usual time of arrival there in the month of September. As to the extent of largeness of this island I cannot be particular having only seen it at a great distance to the S.E. of us. In the channel between lays a reef of rock on the Guam side which must be avoided. As to the number of these islands we can only learn that there were reckoned 12 in all and the island Guam being the largest and the southerly most. This is a description of what I have seen which may give a general idea of the situation of the islands, a thing but imperfectly known. We were thus informed besides that at 25 leagues to the northward of the island Ganis lay a tolerable large island called St Augustine which the Manila ship in her passage to Mexico generally makes.

This island is uninhabited and may be known by a volcano on it which frequently burns; as to the seasons we could only learn of the westerly winds which they call the Vandervalls which usually set in about the 24th June N.N.E. This is the stormy rainy season which must be avoided by all ships. This weather continued till the latter end of August when the north east monsoon succeeds and fair weather commences.

The ground was poor for anchoring although under most conditions two anchors appeared to hold fast the Centurion. However from June to September the winds of Tinian are unstable and violent squalls blow up in a matter of minutes. On September 22 Saumarez was on board the ship with a few officers and 108 men (instead of her normal working complement of 400). The Commodore was on shore convalescing in his tent. Saumarez had been suspicious of the weather and the previous day had recalled aboard some of the crew. At 4 pm on the 22nd it blew a fresh gale from the east. The large swells rolling into the anchorage smashed the small pinnace against the stern of the Centurion, and it was hoisted aboard with the utmost difficulty. During the gale one cable parted and the ship swung around on the single anchor that still held. The wind and tide were against each other, creating a confused and dangerous sea. To save the ship Saumarez set her mizzen. Most of the cannons were not lashed down and the top masts and rigging still lay on deck. There had been neither time nor men to look after them. A mountainous sea breaking on the stern threatened to poop the ship. Reefs of rocks ahead about one and a quarter miles away rendered the situation very precarious. The ports were open and the ship was taking water so the fatiguing duty at the pumps began once again. Finally the second anchor cable parted and the Centurion broke loose. Four guns were fired to warn the shore of the danger and signal lights were hoisted. All night the ship was driven out to sea under gale force winds, fortunately clear of the land. By morning the Centurion was four leagues from Tinian and still being uncontrollably blown further west. All the anchor cables but one were cut and dragging overboard, serving to slow down the running ship. The remaining good anchor was pulled aboard.

For five days the gale did not abate. Saumarez first employed the men in saving the main masts, for if they were not properly stayed when the wind changed they would not be able to return. At a break in the weather on September 26, the ship hove-to before setting sail and securing the hatches and top masts that still lay on deck. When this work was done Saumarez then headed the ship back towards the island of Tinian, 'not knowing whether I should not be a captain in spite of my teeth, at last'.

On the first day of October, not sighting the island, Saumarez feared strong westerly currents had set him far off course. However the next day he sighted Guam. From here he could correct his dead reckoning and finally set an accurate course back. Tinian was directly east and he had estimated it to be to the north west. Currents had driven the vessel around almost one hundred and eighty degrees. Contrary winds kept the Centurion beating up to Tinian for nineteen days. Finally on October 10 the southernmost end of the island was thankfully sighted.

When the Centurion was being driven out to sea those left on the island at first felt that the ship would founder on the shoals. But when she was swept clear of the island the violent gales that battered Tinian convinced Anson that the Centurion could not return without her top masts set. If the ship was free of the shoals she would be driven west, perhaps as far as the coast of China. Therefore Anson made immediate plans to meet this contingency.

The captured Spanish bark was cut in half and all the men set to work to lengthen her by twelve feet. The bark would now become a vessel of 140 tons and capable, they all hoped, of a long ocean passage. Canvas tents were cut up into sails, and after searching all their belongings a discarded quadrant and a small compass were finally discovered. Ample provisions were available and the direction of the Chinese coast was known. The plan was to sail to China where they would hopefully meet the Centurion at Macao. Saumarez knew it was their next destination and Anson felt confident that if to return to Tinian was impossible because of wind and sea, Saumarez would undoubtedly sail for the China coast, 1500 miles away. With fresh trade winds now blowing steadily it would be almost impossible to sail back to Tinian against them.

When the Centurion was sighted by Anson and his men a long cheer arose and eighteen seamen were sent off with provisions to meet the ship. As the Centurion came slowly to anchor in Tinian harbour Anson was the first man aboard to greet his lieutenant. The normally reserved Anson, who seldom showed his emotions, could not for once disguise his joy. No further time was lost in watering and provisioning with meat and fruit.

During the Centurion's absence two proas had sailed towards shore to reconnoitre the island. No doubt the Spanish were curious as to whether the British ship's departure was permanent. At the approach of the proas the men dismantled their tents and hid, not wishing to be discovered in so vulnerable a state. After several hours of investigation from a safe distance the proas sailed away again, planing over the surface of the sea at up to twenty knots. The swiftness of these native boats continued to astound the English.

The proas were of remarkable construction. The main hull was about 2 feet wide and 34 feet long, made of a hollow log supported by a slim outrigger 10 feet in length. The outrigger was connected to the main hull by means of round struts firmly lashed into place with hemp. Light and well-balanced, it carried a single triangular sail. By rolling the sail around the boom in heavy weather it was able to reef, an ancient forerunner of modern roller-reefing. In the trade winds of the Pacific the proa could glide from one island to another, easily outpacing conventional craft. No sailing vessel has been constructed since to surpass the speed or agility of the Polynesian proa.

The Commodore believed it was now only a matter of days before the governor of Guam decided to act against him. The Spaniards could not tolerate an English presence so close for much longer. In the Centurion's unseaworthy state Anson was not ready to fight. Orders were given to destroy the Spanish bark and all unusable stores and make ready for sea. But on October 13, a fierce unexpected squall once again drove off the Centurion and she dragged her anchor out to sea. This time 70 men were aboard, but most of the others were able to reach the ship by rowing furiously after her in two boats. Somewhere out hunting in the forest were another 40 men. The Centurion was able to come close enough to Tinian three days later to pick up the remainder of her crew. The Indian prisoners were given their freedom and immediately afterwards the Centurion set course for China.

They were in the season of fresh trade winds and this time the Centurion caught them. In spite of a foul bottom and the precarious state of her rigging she logged about 130 miles a day on her way to the China coast. The ship was a mixture of Spanish anchors, relaid ropes, respliced rigging, knotted cordage and newly sewn sails. The crew was English, Spanish, African and Indian. Only constant work at the pumps kept the water below two feet in the bilge. The faster she went the more she laboured and the more the temporarily caulked stern took in the sea. But the men were in fair health and the work did not bother them.

Through the morning haze of November 4, 1742 they sighted the island of Formosa. The ship was now to the west of the island off the Pescadores and steering west by southwest for Macao. At sunrise on the next day they were surprised to find themselves among a flotilla of hundreds of small Chinese sampans that continued to fish without paying the slightest attention to the presence of the giant Centurion. On the following morning they sailed into the midst of an even larger number of sampans which still contemptuously ignored their existence. When one of the sampans began to wave a red flag Saumarez thought at last a pilot had come to lead them safely into Macao. But the red flag was only a signal to the other sampans. The captain of the boat carrying the flag then blew a long horn and all the fishing craft suddenly hauled in their nets and left the fishing ground.

The Centurion picked her way on down the coast alone while the ubiquitous sampans silently continued to encircle the man-of-war, until at last Anson anchored in the Great West Channel at the entrance to the Canton River, still over twenty miles from Macao.

Unexpectedly not one but three pilots came alongside and said they would gladly guide the vessel to Macao. One was chosen. Communication took place in Portuguese and

Saumarez agreed to pay thirty dollars for the service. That morning the British learned that there were four East Indiamen, one Country, two French, two Dutch and two Danish ships anchored in the Canton River. But it took four days of tedious beating upstream before the Centurion came to rest at her anchorage in Macao Road.

CHAPTER TWELVE: MACAO

The colony of Macao was held by the Portuguese under tolerance from the Chinese to whom substantial rental was paid. Macao was a small fortress, weak and relatively ineffective but the only foreign colony the Chinese would permit. Until Anson arrived the Chinese Mandarins treated all foreigners with a general haughty contempt. Foreigners were uncivilised and inferior. They were heathens. If the Hoppo, the Mandarin in charge of the colony, so chose, he could close the gate to the city. The Portuguese colony would then be cut off from the mainland and at the mercy of the officials. This had happened more than once — when the small settlement was almost starved to death for not cooperating with the Chinese.

Since the late 17th century the Portuguese had built factories to store goods that were used in the trade between Europeans and the Chinese. The Chinese were tremendously industrious and ingenious. They were great traders, shrewd, imperious and lived according to customs that involved elaborate ceremony. Authority in minute detail, assiduously obeyed, was implicit in the system. All Hoppos were undisputed masters of their territory but were in turn obsequious in their obedience to the Chantuk or Viceroy at Canton. The present Chantuk gave his unquestioned allegiance to the Emperor Kien-Lung at Peking.

The British East India traders could only deal with other Chinese traders who arranged everything for them through the Hoppos. The system was paternal and operated with the benefit of large bribes. At Canton, the Viceroy had never yet been seen by any foreigner. He kept aloof from the traders who plied between China and Europe in the pursuit of their business. Nor had a man-of-war of any nation entered the Canton River. The Chinese mind worked in a way that was truly mysterious to the European. Neither understood the thinking of the other and the one common bond that held them together was money. The Centurion had not come to China to trade and this confused the Chinese. It made them more, rather than less, suspicious.

The Centurion required considerable attention. Her bottom, deck and rigging needed a complete overhaul and sails had to be replaced. Provisions of every kind were in short supply. After all this was done the man-of-war would ostensibly make sail for Batavia in the East Indies and then England. But the plan was that as soon as the ship was ready they would head in total secrecy for Macao Cape Espirito Santo, near Manila, to lay in wait for the galleon. However, before any negotiations could begin with the Chinese certain protocol had to be followed.

The Centurion was riding comfortably at anchor on November 15, 1742 in the bay of Teipe Quebrado five miles off Macao. Being unfamiliar with the tides the vessel had been accidentally grounded in the mud since early morning and it was not before 4 pm that she refloated. When a small breeze sprang up the fore topsails were set and she ran to a new anchoring place where there would be sufficient water during low tide. It was at Macao that Saumarez corrected his account of time, suddenly realising in the relative quiet of their anchorage that he had lost a day by circumnavigating the globe in a westerly direction.

That morning the Commodore sent one of his officers to see the governor of Macao in his fortress to settle some matters of protocol. Anson was anxious to establish his presence immediately as a commander of a naval man-of-war with all the rights that were attendant upon his position. The British officer was to inform the Portuguese governor that the Commodore would salute the castle at Macao if the governor would promise to return his salute with an equal number of guns. At noon on the next day the British officer returned in his boat from his visit with the Portuguese governor. The governor promised to salute the Commodore as was appropriate to his rank. When the Commodore landed at Macao it was further agreed that eleven guns would welcome him at the fortress. Shortly afterwards the fortress was saluted with eleven guns and a short time later a like number of cannons boomed out from Macao. The first part of the ceremony amicably settled, the Commodore then hired a Chinese junk and accompanied by several of his officers went off to the city of Canton to solicit the Viceroy for supplies and carpenters to refit the ship. In his absence Saumarez took command.

The Canton River was a place of intense activity and Saumarez observed with great interest the numerous Chinese sampans bringing large quantities of cheap hogs, fowl, sheep, ducks, vegetables and fruit so that the entire deck of the Centurion was loaded with food by the end of the day. The food was very necessary for the sailors, most of whom still had the remains of the scurvy in them. The air too was cool and sharp and invigorating, a relief after the incessant heat of the Pacific. Saumarez employed the men in cleaning ship while he awaited word from Anson at Canton. Portuguese, Swedish and Dutch ships passed by sailing further down river to their warehouses at the Chinese city.

When the Hoppo's boat came alongside the Centurion on November 18 and obliged all the Chinese traders passing backwards and forwards on the river to submit to an intensive search, Saumarez had his first taste of Chinese officialdom at work; in the days ahead he was to become more experienced in the complex operation of their bureaucracy. Shortly afterwards Saumarez received an order which came by boat from the Commodore at Canton, instructing him to send a midshipman to the entrance of the harbour to watch for two Spanish ships expected from Manila with money. For this purpose the small boats were to be kept ready for sea should the Manila ships appear. No doubt Anson picked up this rumour from one of the Indiamen anchored at Canton and he was prepared to take the Spanish ships if he could.

One of the East India merchantmen, the Augusta, had brought mail from England. The squadron was optimistically expected to arrive in Macao about this time. There was personal mail for most of the officers. They now all learned of the return of the Severn and Pearle to Buenos Aires. It had been assumed that both these vessels had perished along with the Wager on the rocks of Patagonia. There seemed to be little comment either personal or official on the return of either of these ships. It could be argued that if four members of the squadron, one of which was the Anna, were able to reach Chile, then the Severn and Pearle were also capable of succeeding. But there were too many immediate problems to waste time arguing about a matter that now belonged in the past. Yet the crew of the Centurion all knew that had they arrived in the Southern Ocean with a slightly larger force they could have dominated the Pacific.

It was quite clear that the Centurion's presence in China was an acute embarrassment to the East Indiamen and the governor of Macao. One of the East India supercargoes in Canton, writing on December 14, 1742 to his headquarters in London reflected the attitude of the other English merchants.

'We have nothing of moment to acquaint you of, having found the government as usual in transacting our business, till the arrival of Mr Anson on the 18th of last month in a distressed condition with his ship. He has given the Chinese merchants a great deal of trouble, and occasioned our delay, none of the officers of the government caring to undertake the granting of a chop for his refitting and victualling, as he is not upon a footing with merchant ships, and pays no port charges. A King's ship coming being without precedent. Everybody avoided being concerned in the affair and the merchants at last proposed the shipping of some provisions on board our ships to be delivered off Macao to get Mr Anson from Canton, who would not stir until he had surety of getting some.' The East Indiamen also feared for the safety of their Chinese merchants who 'would lose their heads' should Anson take a Spanish ship near Macao.

Anson as the commander of a King's ship stubbornly refused to pay harbour dues. The Portuguese governor of Macao, anxious to avoid trouble, was thus forced to move the Centurion to a new anchorage on the Taypa where no dues were required. But it was soon apparent that the governor of Macao wielded no power and was little more than a puppet of the Chantuk in Canton. The governor apologised but he could offer no provisions nor did he have facilities to hire men to repair the Centurion. In spite of Anson's great perplexity at meeting English merchants who put business before country, he was nevertheless resolved not to injure England's trading interests with China.

The Commodore wished only to repair and victual his ship. His requests were simple and his direct mind could not understand why this should disturb anyone. He had money to pay or overpay, if necessary. But the presence of a British man-of-war on the Canton River was a frightening event for the Chinese. For the East Indiamen it created complications they could not cope with. The Spanish and French were influential in China and both worked against British interests. The solution to the Centurion's problems required the talents of a diplomat combined with the veiled threats of a soldier who could back them up if necessary. Fortunately, this was available. At first Anson heeded the cautious fears of the English merchants in dealing with the Chinese. But both he and Saumarez, who was to conduct most of the negotiations, were still novices. The Commodore also hoped that some of the supernumary officers anxious to leave for home could exchange themselves for badly needed sailors on the British India ships.

December 2nd 1742. Moored at Taipa Quebrado
Moderate and hazy. At 2 PM. a long boat arrived from Wampo, the place where the English China ships lay. This boat the Commodore purchased from the Augusta commanded by Captain Townshend, with an anchor of 30 hundredweight and a new cable of 1 ½ inches and 28 pounds of wine; the whole furniture of the boat was included which was well found. In the morning manned her with the boat crew of our own and sent her up to Wampo to bring down more purchased stores. We likewise received the boatswain of the Augusta who was warranted for his ship by the Commodore. Bent one of our cables to this new anchor.

December 3rd 1742. Moored at Taipa Quebrado
Hazy, the middle and the latter blew fresh gales and rain. Took 1020 dollars out of a chest marked number 2 by

order of the Commander to send to Canton to buy stores.

December 10th 1742. Moored at Taipa Quebrado
The first part fresh gales and close, the latter moderate and fair. AM. longboat went to Canton having most of the Gloucester's officers in her, who went to try if they could get men from the India ships in lieu having leave from the Commodore on these terms to go for England. The Defence's long boat went likewise having with her our sprung main topmast and one of the Prize's main yards. At 8 got up the foreyard and topmast and got the topsail yard and the ga'tsail yard across.

After an unsuccessful visit to the Portuguese governor to obtain carpenters and sea-stores it was decided that Saumarez would be left in charge of the Centurion while the Commodore would proceed again up to Canton to visit the Chantuk. Anson would be accompanied by a retinue of sailors and several barges that he hoped would suitably impress the Viceroy. The purpose was to see the man at the top since none of the local Hoppos had authority to hire the carpenters for the repair of the Centurion, nor instruct Chinese merchants to sell the vast quantities of food needed for an ocean voyage.

Before Anson's departure the local Hoppo came alongside the Centurion in his barge in a state of great excitement and told Anson that he needed a permit to go up the Canton River and that the permit would not be granted. Saumarez then gave instructions to the Centurion's frightened interpreter. While the sailors stood by in a menacing mood the answer was given to the Chinese official. Unless Commodore Anson of the Royal Navy was granted the permit to proceed to Canton on the following morning, he would arm all his men in the longboat and go up the river without a permit. If anyone dared stop one of His Majesty's ships on her journey they would do so at their peril. The Hoppo had a good look around at the ship's armament and hurriedly parted with all his retinue in two junks to report back to the Viceroy.

The next morning word was sent to the Commodore that the permit had been granted. This example of British gunboat diplomacy on the Canton River would not be unusual in the coming century. The permit being granted Anson immediately set off in his longboat the seventy miles up river to the city, ordering Saumarez to make the ship ready for a quick departure since the unfriendly Chinese in collusion with the French could be a threat to their safety. After several days of waiting near Canton aboard the Augusta, Anson was denied permission to see the Chantuk.

The merchants continued to urge caution, protesting that their livelihood was at stake. But the truth was rather of a different character. If a British naval ship was to be given preferential treatment and the Commodore was to have an audience with the Chantuk, the East India captains would lose that most precious of all commodities in China: face. To lose face would do incalculable harm. Yielding to the advice of the Company merchants Anson wrote a letter to one of the principal Chinese dealers, who had agreed to act as intermediary and carry his letter directly to the Chantuk in his royal palace at Canton. However, it was discovered later that the letter was never delivered.

The East India captains did everything they could to get rid of the Centurion. The quickest way they thought was to provide what was necessary. But they miscalculated on the resoluteness of the men they were dealing with. In the same way certain conceptions were utterly beyond the astute Mandarins. Anson wrote to his friend James Naish from Canton in December: 'They told us that the Mandarins had such a strange notion of a ship which went about the world seeking other ships in order to take them, and they could not be brought to hear reason on that head.'

The Mandarins assumed that the singular object of the Centurion was to accumulate treasure without trade, and they were not far wrong, but this concept astounded them. The Chinese accumulated treasure by judicious dealings which required no risk to life. Their battles were won over the bartering tables without guns. The Commodore at last believed he understood the true nature of events and decided to take matters into his own hands. He formally wrote to the head of the East India merchantmen requesting supplies. In times of peril, he pointed out, the merchantmen sought the protection of His Majesty's Navy. Now one of His Majesty's ships was in dire need and required assistance.

An agreement was made supposedly without Chinese knowledge, to load the Centurion from East Indiamen that were homeward bound. Over 2000 pounds of bread and 120 bushels of pulse and several thousand pounds of pork were transferred to the Centurion during December and January; probably with the silent assent of the Chinese, who did not want a direct confrontation with Anson. Meanwhile, there was an active secret correspondence up and down the Canton River between Anson and Saumarez, planning the strategy for their campaign. This was carried from the Centurion to Anson, quartered by Captain Townshend in the Augusta near Canton.

It was arranged that Captain Saunders, who had commanded the Tryall, was to return to England in one of the East India ships. He was entrusted with Anson's Letter of Proceedings to the Admiralty which in effect was a summary of the logs of Saumarez.

The Reverend Richard Walter managed to return home as well. He was anxious to be the first in print with his book of the voyage, published in 1748, which became a best seller of the day. We now know a large part of this book came from Saumarez' journals. Colonel Cracherode of the Marines was sent off by Anson with gracious thanks for his services. There were no more Royal Marines left to command.

The delays were indeed frustrating. But as days passed into weeks slowly progress was made in provisioning the ship. However, the East Indiamen adamantly refused to trade able-bodied seamen for Anson's extra officers. Fortunately, there was still adequate crew to work the Centurion. But without sea supplies and a sound ship they could not make the extended voyage that lay ahead. The survivors had not come this far to peacefully acquiesce to a death sentence dictated by the Viceroy at Canton. The clandestine supplies given by the East India Company were offered in the hope that the Commodore would cause no more trouble and quietly depart. But this was not to be. Anson sent a letter to Saumarez, enclosing a demand written in Chinese for all the stores required. Saumarez was to take this letter immediately to the Portuguese governor at Macao who was to instruct the local Hoppo in his presence to deliver it to the Viceroy at Canton. Anson wanted to make one more peaceful attempt to obtain his requirements before he resorted to more desperate measures.

After several days and many delays a meeting was arranged between Saumarez and the Hoppo in Macao. In unequivocal terms Saumarez impressed upon the Hoppo that the letter was to be delivered personally to the Viceroy. The English man-of-war was in critical need of repair. On December 16 Anson returned to the Centurion to wait for results.

December 16th 1742. Moored at Taipa Quebrado
Moderate weather intermixed with small amount of rain. This afternoon the Commodore returned from Canton without success in regard to obtaining a chop or commission to careen the ship but with much difficulty he got some dry provisions which were put on board the Indian ships in order to bring down to us; the ships being expected daily. Received 686 lbs of pork from the agents which we have salted up for the sea store; received by the Defence's long boat with one coil of 5 inch rope and 2 pieces of rope for stays.

December 17th 1742. Moored at Taipa Quebrado
8 AM. our long boat returned from Canton with 3 ½ bags and 3 chests of bread and 20 bags of calavances. Received 378 lbs of beef and 1,082 lbs of pork from the agent, most part of which was salted up. The carpenter employed in overhauling and fixing new rigging. Caulked the foremast, lower deck ports in the ship, being ready for the sea.

December 18th 1742. Moored at Taipa Quebrado
24 hours moderate and fair. PM. unbent foretopsail and bent another. AM. opened all the lower deck ports and ran the guns out in expectation of being visited by a Chinese Mandarin. Accordingly at 10 he came on board attended by several row boats resembling half galleys. We received them with drum beating and a guard drawn out, his design being to inform himself whether we were

a King's ship or one who had assumed the title and make his report to the Chantuk or Viceroy of Canton; our careening depending on the result of this visit. Received 1212 lbs of pork for sea use.

December 19th 1742. Moored at Taipa Quebrado
First part moderate and fair. 3 PM. saluted the Mandarin at his going with 15 guns. At 5 discerned two of the India ships coming into the Road early in the morning. Two long boats were sent on board to bring the provisions, but blowing too hard one of them was unable to fetch the ships and put back. Took two thousand dollars out of the box number 2 being the Carmela's Prize money for the use of the ship.

December 20th 1742. Moored at Taipa Quebrado
These 24 hours it blew very fresh with drifting rain. PM. the long boat returned from the Augusta India ship with some of the Commodore's things. Then two longboats attempted to go back for provisions but were put back. AM. lowered the yards. Observed we had started our anchors.

December 24th 1742. Moored at Taipa Quebrado
At 5 PM. a Dutch ship passing by from Canton bound for Batavia. We sent the boat on board her to endeavour to purchase stores which she refused selling, but sold one coil of 4 inch and another 2 ½ inch. Weighed the small bower and new moored the ship. AM. sent our long boat to Canton to get some more stores from the India ships there. Our men employed in overhauling the rigging and mending the sails.

December 25th 1742. Moored at Taipa Quebrado
Moderate and fair these 24 hours. PM. a Portuguese ship anchored here from Macao and saluted us with 5 guns returned three. Received £334 of beef from the agent, the carpenter being sent to Macao to purchase some deales returned with 27,13 ft long.

December 27th 1742. Moored at Taipa Quebrado
Moderate intermixed with rain. AM. two Danes India ships past by and saluted us, the one with 11 and the other with 9 guns, return'd two less to each. Received £260 beef from the agents. Employed in fitting the rigging.

December 28th 1742. Moored at Taipa Quebrado
First part moderate the latter fresh gales with much rain. Receiv'd £296 beef from the agent. Employed as before.

December 29th 1742. Moored at Taipa Quebrado
Uncertain squally weather with rain. Receiv'd from the agent £342 beef and 4 hogs live; were obliged to have the hogs brought on board alive to prevent the Chinese defrauding us, having observed that they injected water into them to render them weightier, besides which it rendered the meat unfit for salting.

December 30th 1742. Moored at Taipa Quebrado
These 24 hours proved more moderate. The carpenter purchased in Macao 22 boards, 4 pieces of timber to repair the pinnace. The men employed in overhauling

and fitting the new rigging. Converted 45 yards of an old maintopsail to make hammocks for the people.

January 1st 1743. Moored at Taipa Quebrado
The same weather. PM. our long boat returned from Canton and brought from the India ship one long anchor of 28 hundredwt with one pump, one barrel of tar and 9 shovels. Received £502 of beef, £288 of pork from the agent; a boat load of wood came on board.

January 2nd 1743. Moored at Tapia Quebrado
24 hours generally blew fresh. A large Portuguese ship stopped and anchored near us from Macao.

January 3rd 1743. Moored at Taipa Quebrado
Moderate and fair the whole part. Men employed in examining the rigging.

January 4th 1743. Moored at Taipa Quebrado
The first part moderate and fair the latter fresh gales and hazy, waiting with great impatience to know of the results of the Mandarin's visit. There being great consultations at Canton on the subject.

January 5th 1743. Moored at Taipa Quebrado
The same weather as before. The ship's company being in want of money to supply themselves with necessaries made the application to the Commodore and having unanimously chosen him agent a division was made of the Payta Prize money; the Tryalls and we being captors accordingly was divided amounting to three thousand dollars. The Commodore sharing, the commissioned

officers 500 the warrant officers 300, the midshipmen and inferior officers 63 and the foremastmen 33 dollars; this morning the Hoppo at Macao sent by one of his officers a permission (or what they call a Grand Chop) wherein we were allowed liberty to purchase what necessaries we wanted for careening and likewise to hire their junks or vessels for the service and the carpenters and caulkers — the limited time being 20 days to perform the work in, but if it was not sufficient to be prolonged by the Hoppo after which we were to depart from their kingdom.

January 6th 1743. Moored at Taipa Quebrado
Hazy this evening. I was ordered to Canton to hire one or two junks according to their bigness and buy rigging canvas, oil, oakum and iron, having 2000 dollars to pay for what I bespoke. Accordingly I hired a Chinese boat at Macao and pursued my journey. Were supplied with 484 pounds of beef by the agent.

The Commodore and his first officer ceremoniously escorted the Mandarins through the Centurion on December 18 and had undoubtedly impressed them. Until the last moment the Mandarins had kept everyone in suspense before granting permission for the chop. The Commodore commenting on the Hoppo's visit wrote to James Naish from Macao: 'After I had satisfied his [the Mandarin's] inquiries he told me my case was to be heard before the Chantuk Fooyen and Grand Hoppo Man, and that he was my advocate. He dined with me and stayed aboard five hours which gave me the opportunity of making him the master of my case.' They dined on beef and chicken which the Chinese ate with difficulties since they had never seen knives nor forks before. Anson apologised for the humble fare explaining the variety of his food had been severely limited by the Chinese. He could do no better. But the Chinese drank copiously from the Commodore's fine wines, and after consuming over a bottle each were still apparently in full possession of their senses. After the meal Anson 'sent him away well satisfied and he assured me he would do me all the service in his power and did not doubt that everything I desired would be granted. I believe he did his utmost, but the judges gave it against us and we were legally condemned to perish by hunger! But the Grand Hoppo was not only one of the bench but highly bribed to be advocate against my Mandarin; asked him with a sneer what he thought I would do upon receiving a refusal of my demands, which raised a curiosity in the Vice-King to inquire whether he had informed himself from me. He said I had told him that in case I received a refusal (which I thought impossible) I should then consult with my people whether to eat one another or the Chinese, and that I desired to put himself in my circumstances and consider whose lot he thought it would fall to! Upon which the Viceroy declared that I must be supplied and that he would take it upon himself to answer it to the Emperor, and immediately issued out a proclamation through the Province that all the Chinese were at liberty to furnish me with what I wanted.'

It was a new Chinese experience to meet with men who were quite uninterested in trade and who had a higher loyalty to King and country. But the armament of the Centurion was also too impressive to be ignored. There was a quality of courteous toughness in the Commodore and his first lieutenant that the Mandarins were unsure how to assess. It seemed that the danger from this British man-of-war was by far greater than the rewards from all the bribes that French East Indiamen could offer, and his first lieutenant that the Mandarins were unsure Once permission was granted by the Viceroy to commence work hundreds of Chinese workmen appeared, swarming over the ship like ants. They began by replacing planks, recaulking the bottom and sides and re-sheathing. The Chinese were highly skilled craftsmen and rapid workers, but nevertheless the deadline set by the Hoppo would not allow sufficient time for completion.

It remained clear that the necessary materials, labour and stores were controlled by the Chinese, and that the foreign traders were acting in their own interests. The local contractors meant to profit from their advantageous position.

Samuel Scott's oil painting of the Centurion taking the Cobadonga

January 10th 1743. New moored with the ship at Taipa Quebrado

Moderate and cloudy. At 1 PM. a Chinese Mandarin came on board attended with several row boats. This person was governor of the district in which Macao was included. His residence being at a small town called Tansong, at 16 lgs off from whence we were to be supplied with carpenters. He came on board to settle the number we wanted and to exhort us to be very expeditious else we should loose the northerly monsoon, and partly likewise to receive a present. At his leaving us, we saluted him with 15 guns. 7 PM. moored the ship in a ¼ less 6 fms.

January 14th 1743. Moored at Taipa Quebrado
The same weather, our long boat brought on board from Macao 20 spars, 35 plank, and two knees which we borrowed from one of the merchants, on condition of paying a settled price, in case they were lost or broken. Designing this timber, with more that was to come, to build stages with which to carry our stores on to be put in a store house on the island. Made 73 hammocks for our people from a part of our old sails.

January 15th 1743. Moored at Taipa Quebrado
Same weather. Received from Macao 7 large planks and one piece of fir for chocks. AM. a company ship belonging to the Portuguese sailed hence for Lisbon and saluted us with 9 guns. We return'd the same number being informed she was on the establishment of the King's ship. Our men employed in knotting and drawing yarn.

January 16th 1743. Moored at Taipa Quebrado
Continuing moderate and fair. Sent several of our men to the island we lay near in order to clear and smooth the ground where we intended to build our shore house

which is here called a banghazar consisting of spars or large bamboos and cover'd over with mats. Received 209 pds of beef from the agent.

January 19th 1743. Moored at Taipa Quebrado
Same weather. Received from the agents two butts of spirituous liquor called lamshee, resembling very bad arrack, there being no quantity of arrack to be purchased this year. 28 Chinese caulkers came on board and began to caulk the starboard side.

January 20th 1743. Moored at Taipa Quebrado
Fresh gales and hazy. Sent ashore our booms and spars and cleared our decks of all our lumber. Sent our pinnace and cutter to be hauled up ashore which were much out of repair. 48 caulkers employed on board but a far greater number were expected soon. Agreed to give them 2,000 dollars for careening and completing the ship entirely; this was esteemed a very extravagant price in these parts where day labour is extremely cheap but there was no remedy; they were besides to be supplied with firing and fresh water and huts to lodge in. On the island the Chinese employed in building the banghazar.

January 26th 1743. Moored at Taipa Quebrado
The weather more moderate and fair than formerly. AM. two junks arrived which I had hired at Canton the largest of about 150 tuns for 500 takell or £167 sterling the other of 90 tuns for 250 takells or £83 6sh. 8d sterling. Esteeming each takell at 6 sh. 8d sterling. Having in them 152 yards of canvas for small sails with some cotton cloth; 4 hundredweight of iron for working

up and 240 pds of this country oakum which is beat and shredded out of bamboo or cane.

January 27th 1743. Moored at Taipa Quebrado
Moderate and hazy these 24 hours PM. I returned on board from Canton having bespoke for most of what was necessary. The cordage which was the principal thing I contracted for at 9 takells a pekull, each pekull weighing 12pds. They being obliged to bring it on board with 30 ½ tubs of oyle amounting to 100 pekulls and at 5 takell per pekull. 4 pekull of iron at 2 takells, 5 mace (a mace is the decimal of a takell) 50 pekull of stoppade bamboo or oakum at 4 takells per pekull. 8 pekull of canvas at 22 takells per pekull. 20 cadey of twine at 2 mace, 5 candarines per cadey. Each cadey amounting to 16 02. and a candarine is the 10th pt. of a mace; 18 sheaves of 22 inches diameter and 3 ½ ins. thick at 3 takells 5 mace per sheave. 2 baskets of darner (which is a gross of turpentine) at 1 takell 5 mace per pekull. Employed in sending our rigging and provisions ashore. 20 more caulkers on board.

January 29th 1743. Moored at Taipa Quebrado
Fresh gales and cloudy. Sending all our stores and provisions ashore. 100 Chinese caulkers came on board to complete the ship.

While the ship was careened she was a vulnerable target for the enemy. Now was the time to set upon her. All ballast, treasure, guns, powder and shot were put onto the junks and carried to the banghazar. On February 18 when the ship lay helpless the local Mandarin ordered the caulkers ashore saying the time limit had expired. Only after vociferous protests was work continued and the Chinese ordered back. Then the carpenters completed stripping off the copper sheathing and started to replace the rotted planks.

February 25th 1743. Moored at Taipa Quebrado

Good weather. At 6 P.M. weighed the ship and in the morning early hove out as far as yesterday's worke and clapt on new sheathing, painting it as we sheathed with a mixture called chinam, it being this bamboo oakum beat up with a particular oyle (call'd leppe oyle) and whiten'd it with lime: this resembles mortar which they clap on with their hands and smooth it with a piece of leather dip't in water, it being a long time hardening after which it becomes a strong terrass, and the Portuguese sailed with it for three years without renewing it. This cement was clap't on both the ship's bottom and on the sheathing. The bottom we found everywhere very sound excepting a few butt heads which required new driving.

By the end of the first week in March 1743, the repairs to the Centurion were finished and the guns, powder and treasure were placed aboard once more. It had been a precarious time.

News had reached the Commodore that the Spaniards waiting 700 miles away in Manila were acquainted with the condition of the last ship of the squadron. A French captain had volunteered for 40,000 Spanish dollars to attack the immobilised Centurion and crew, but the treasure chest of the Spanish Viceroy was empty and the money could not be found. While the Spanish treasury may have been empty in Manila, their galleons were not. Forty thousand dollars would have been a small price to pay for the death of the Centurion.

Spanish lack of foresight was to cost them dearly in the days to come.

March 10th 1743. Moored at Taipa Quebrado
Moderate and fair. Employ'd as yesterday. Had another false alarm, the pinnace and cutter chasing a Portuguese snow that sailed from hence. But in the morning a Chinese fisherman brought us intelligence that he had been on board a large Spanish ship laying off the Ladrone Islands; that there were two more smaller vessels in company. He had brought one of the officers ashore at Macao from whence early in the morning boats went off to them with others, desiring no money if what he alleged was false. This gave us apprehension it was an armament from Manila against us on which the pinnace was sent out to give our two boats advice of it in order to look out strictly, and we on board saw our guns, small arms and all things in a posture of defence. Unrigged the main mast and got the new shrouds over. The Mandarin with much persuasion permitted 30 of the carpenters to assist us in finishing the ship and in fishing the foremast.

March 13th 1743. Moored at Taipa Quebrado
Same weather as before. Employ'd as before; our pinnace returned having given our other two boats intelligence who still stayed out but had seen nothing; that the whole was a falsity. Got the main topmast through the capstan and rigged him; receiv'd from Macao a square piece of timber 87 ft. long and 13 inches through, for the foremast.

April 3rd 1743. Moored at Taipa Quebrado

Hard squalls with much thunder. Later grew more moderate. Employ'd in making up our booms, clearing the decks and rendering the ship fit for sea. Brought at Macao a cable of 10 ½ inches 95 fathoms long, beginning to unlay him to bolt rope a new main and fore topsail we were making with the strands. Two Mandarin's boats anchored here from Macao being very urgent with us to go away and refusing to assist us with any more necessaries or refreshments, forbidding all the Chinese from coming on board or even selling us anything in the market. The coolies and carpenters were ordered away from us on this occasion.

On April 11, 1743 the Centurion began warping out of the Canton River, but it was not until the 18th that she was clear of the shoals and free of the tides and mud banks. In the process of leaving she lost her cutter and one of her bowers. She saluted the castle at Macao with 19 guns, and the governor with careful attention to protocol returned the salute with the same number. The harbour boomed with the echoes of the explosions as the Centurion with all her sails set tacked out of the channel. Officially she was bound for Batavia and England around the Cape of Good Hope, although the monsoon season was dangerously advanced for any East Indies voyage.

On board there were now 237 men, officers and boys in reasonable health. Twenty three Lascars, Dutch and Indians had been recruited while in Macao. The ship felt solid again and there was a sense of well-being among officers and men as the Centurion cut through the long Pacific swells.

CHAPTER THIRTEEN: CAPTURE OF THE SPANISH TREASURE GALLEON

After several days at sea the Commodore assembled the entire crew on the quarter deck and told them that they were not going to Batavia. Instead, it was his intention to cruise for the Spanish treasure ship off Cape Espiritu Santo in the Philippines. And this time they meant to capture her.

The news was greeted with cheers. Only the capture of the galleon could justify all the hardships and disappointments of the voyage. Stories circulated that the galleon's sides were constructed of such thick oak that she was impenetrable. But Anson was confident that his twenty four 24-pounders at close range could shatter any Spanish hull.

There were few dangers left that could frighten the tough survivors of the squadron. They had endured, it seemed, every peril that a cruel ocean voyage could impose. The Spaniards in the Pacific were meanwhile living a life of *mañana*. No one was in a hurry to make any decision even where life and fortune were at stake. The Spanish governor of Guam knew the Centurion was being refitted and was conscious of her intention to seek out the galleon. But the intelligence apparently did not unduly disturb him.

A small Spanish man-of-war, the Pilar, was being equipped to accompany the Nuestra Señora de Cobadonga for protection, but she was not ready in time. Although the galleon was carrying great treasure, the governor of Manila thought 530 men and sixty guns an adequate argument against the considerably smaller crew of the Centurion. The Spaniards seemed to be trusting in providence to take care of them. The

British, on the other hand, were engaging constantly in target practice off the Philippine coast. They put their faith in their 24-pounders and a special squad of sharp-shooters under command of Jacob Blackbeard, who would be lying high up on the topyards aiming down onto the deck of the galleon once she was within range. Every gun aboard the Centurion would be put to use when the time came.

By April 21 the Centurion was steadily plying to the eastward, bearing well clear of the north-east end of the island of Luconia to avoid being discovered by the Spaniards. Soundings taken day and night told Saumarez they were sailing through water free of shoals and that the sea bed was composed of soft mud. With the inadequate charts available it was always possible they would find themselves in shallow water where it might be necessary to drop anchor suddenly in unfavourable winds as they cruised among the many small islands off the Philippines. Two anchors had been lost at Tinian and replaced from an East Indiaman on the Canton River. When the anchors were inspected on April 21 it was discovered that the stream anchor had broken in half. Saumarez recorded that on discovering the damage they lashed the broken one to two smaller anchors to make a single one weighing 4000 pounds. This and a sheet anchor was all the ship had. Since they were sounding in 65 fathoms there was always the possibility they would suddenly have to seek refuge from weather. They needed at least two sound anchors for safety. However, the problem of anchors was small compared with the strong currents of which they had no knowledge. Saumarez from his noon sight on April 25 was able to compute his latitude, but the eastings and westings were considered very uncertain. The nights were full of thunder and lightning, and sharp vicious squalls that further confused their dead reckoning. Since the ship kept out of sight of land no bearings could be taken of the few prominent features shown on their old charts.

From the masthead the lookout, at 6 pm on May 1, shouted there was land ahead to the eastward in the shape of a small hill that rose from a grey mist over the horizon. This was assumed to be part of Formosa. Saumarez's reckoning at the time placed them 102 leagues distant from the Grand Ladrones. The lookout thought he saw breakers less than 2 ½ miles away and the ship immediately tacked to stand clear. The breakers posed a puzzling question. Saumarez reported 'tis certain there is no such land laid down in the charts', but the land they saw to the north-east was real and it was no more than 20 miles off.

May 4th 1743. The Grand Ladrone distance 132 leagues 2 miles. Lat 20° 24' N, Lon 243° 22' W
First part fresh gales the latter moderate and fair. At 8 PM. tacked being in some doubt about the Bashee Islands which few of the charts mention and which are imperfectly set down by voyagers; Dampier lays them down in the latt. of 20° 20' N but his observation of the south part of Formosa where we likewise observed differing from ours considerably, makes us suspect his account of the situation. At 12 PM. tacked to the southward and kept a good look out.

May 5th 1743. The Grand Ladrones distance 134 leagues. Lat 21° 27' N, Lon 242° 58' W
Not having an observation for these 2 days past found a difference of 38 min. this day's work between the latt. observed and the latt. by account which must be owing

to the northerly currents. The whole part moderate and clear. 6 PM. tacked and stood to the northward where surrounded with frequent ripplings of current. Discovered at 7 AM. from the masthead five small islands which we took to be the Bashee Islands extending from the east to the south to the South East by South about 10 or 12 leagues distance. At 8 saw one from the deck bearing East South East making like two small homocks. At 11 AM. saw land bearing North ½ West 10 leagues, this by our observation at noon we found was the island of Bothell Tobago Xima and here we had an opportunity of rectifying the mistake in the charts which lay these islands near 25 leagues too far to the westward. By our observation we judged Bothell Tobago Xima to lay in 21° 57' N. latt. At noon the Bashee Islands bore South East by South, 10 leagues distance.

Approaching Cape Espiritu Santo where they were to wait for the galleon powerful currents swept them off course. Charts proved of little help and if they had relied upon them it is possible the Centurion would have foundered on shoals on more than one occasion.

In mid-May the violent motion from great north-east swells broke some of the Centurion's foreyards. When the yards were repaired the men practised gunnery and the sailors who were to man the top yards when the galleon was sighted, exercised their small arms on targets that were placed on the water. When the gunnery practice was over a puncheon of captured Spanish brandy containing 73 gallons was broken open and served to the crew to quiet the general excitement at the prospect of soon meeting the treasure galleon. On May 17 in extremely hot weather, stripped to the waist, the men continued their gunnery while new steering sails were prepared by the sailmakers. Muskets, small arms and the great guns were all in readiness.

On May 19 Saumarez judged himself to be in the latitude of 13° N which was the approximate parallel of Cape Espiritu Santo where they would wait for the treasure ship. The Centurion had at last arrived for her fateful rendezvous.

May 20th 1743. Tobago Xima distance 201 leagues. Lat 12° 41' N, Lon 239° 17' W

At ½ past noon saw land from the masthead bearing South West ½ West, 11 or 12 leagues. This by our latitude we judged to be Cape Espiritu Santo, though by our charts esteemed ourselves 3 leagues to the eastward of it which we rather esteemed erroneous than our reckonings not having found any currents by our observations. This error seems likewise the more probable as we found the Bashee Islands laid down 25 leagues too westerly; on seeing the land we tacked and took in our topga'tsail to prevent being discovered. At 4 PM. it bore South West distance 11 leagues. It appeared of a moderate height with several round homocks on it. We judged we saw the pitch of the Cape nor discerning any more land to the northward but saw several homocks rising to the southward. From our observation at noon and taking in the bearings of this Cape computed it to lay in 12° 41' N latitude but by our English charts it is laid down in 12° 30' and by the Dutch in 13°. This Cape we proposed to cruise off, keeping between 12° 50' and 13° 5' which with land just discernible from the masthead. The galleons as we are informed always making this land in their passage from Acapulco, this being the southernmost entrance of the Boccadere which leads to Manila, their usual time of arriving being generally about the middle of June. At 6 PM. the Cape bore South West ½ South 8 or 9 leagues. Kept plying on and off. At noon Cape Espiritu Santo bore South West by West 11 leagues distance.

The meeting with the Cobadonga was almost predetermined. It was inevitable, and every man saw the squalor of his life enriched forever by gold. The Spaniards on their side had been convinced by their officers that the crew of the Centurion was so undermanned and weak that they could not possibly defend themselves. Don Geronimo Montero, general and captain of the Cobadonga, was filled with false confidence by the governor of Manila. Reports from spies in Macao and elsewhere confirmed that the British were a ragged, piratical gang sailing an unseaworthy ship. Until the time of the encounter this was believed to be true. Without this excuse it is difficult to offer any logical explanation for the behaviour of the Spaniards.

A new moon on June 11 created currents that pulled the ship closer to land so that Saumarez saw the tree lined rocky shore of the coast. The chance of discovery by the lookouts on the Cape was a constant hazard. But the Spaniards, unknown to the English, had long since detected their presence, which in no way seemed to deter the galleon. The Nuestra Señora de Cobadonga did not change her plans.

June 20th 1743. Cape Espiritu Santo West South West 8 or 9 leagues

At sunrise we were agreeably surprised with the sight of a sail from the masthead in the South East quarter, her top gallant sails appearing half out of the horizon. We naturally concluded it must be one of the galleons, and made no doubt of seeing the other soon. On which we unlashed the lower deck guns, and prepared all things for engaging. At ½ past 7 we discerned the ship off the deck, her topsails being half out of the water, and observed the smoke of the gun she fired, and at the same time took in her top gallant. We likewise fired a gun to leeward in order to amuse and distract them, but judged her gun was a signal to her consort to hasten to her, though we learnt afterwards from them that they imagined we had been a small vessel which is generally sent from Manila to furnish them with cables and anchors. At 10 we wore to northward to intercept her. At 11 had her hull entirely out of the horizon, and not seeing any other ship began to think she had lost company by some accident, but were surprised to see her bear down to us so boldly. At ½ past 11 she hauled her foresail up, and brought to under topsails with her head to the northward; and hoisted Spanish colours and the standard at the main topgallant masthead. At noon we lowered our long boat down and ran out the starboard lower deck guns, which we pointed to the object, the chase being about two points on the starboard bow and three miles off. During these intervals we had several squalls of wind and rain which often obscured the chase, but whenever it cleared up observed her resolutely laying to. At 7 past noon we took in the topgallant sails and hauled the mainsail up, and soon after hoisted the broad pendant and colours and fired such of the chase and bow guns from alow and aloft as could be brought to bear on her; and got our spiritsail fore and aft. The galleon immediately returned our fire with two of his stern chasers which he plyed briskly, and likewise rigged his spiritsail yard fore and aft. His shot were not ill directed, and generally shattered our rigging. As we observed he had no lower tier of guns we were amazed to think what he could propose against our weight of metal and a ship of our appearance; but we learnt afterwards that they depended on their superior number of men, which indeed far exceeded ours, he having 550 men on board and from the accounts received at Acapulco knew that when we left that coast we had not above 200.

Being come abreast of him within pistol shot, the engagement began on both sides with great briskness. Our guns during the whole time being loaded with ball and grapeshot made great havoc, as likewise our tops which were full of our best marksmen, by the enemy's own confession galled them extremely. Our first broadside had a good effect both with his men and rigging. His ensign staff amongst other things was shot away, then the ensign set on fire, but was soon extinguished by them. The enemy on his side kept plying us with his guns and pedros, the latter being loaded with bags of stones, iron nails and musket ball quartered as for the musketeers. After the first discharge of them they were observed seldom to appear, our grape scouring the decks very successfully. After near an hour's space we observed their fire to abate considerably, and being within three boat lengths of each other could observe the officers running about confusedly as if they were preventing the desertion of their men from their quarters, which accordingly proved so. As from the beginning we had an entire contempt of the enemy we could arrogate to ourselves no merit in the continuance of our fire, and indeed our guns began to heat considerably, recoiling with such force as broke most of their breechings, which might be chiefly owing to the mixed natures. After near two hours engagement from our first gun he struck his standard, and soon after his jack, and within a few minutes after fell on the starboard quarter, but bearing him clear he fell astern, and we hoisted the cutter out, the Commodore sending me on board to take possession of her and send him the principal officers. At my arrival on board I found them in that state of mind the conquered may generally be supposed to be in, being doubtful of the treatment they were to receive, and at the same time had no great opinion of our humanity from the different persuasions in religion, having represented us to themselves as a set of cannibals which the priests take care to inculcate, especially with the Indians. But having complimented them on their behaviour and resolute resistance I assured them of such quarters and useage as their bravery deserved, and sent them on board the Commodore as fast as I possibly could, the weather looking very windy. I having but ten persons on board a ship that appeared crowded with men. But by 8 in the evening had sent away 300 prisoners, and was reinforced from the Commodore with 40 men and officers, that in all we mustered up 50.

Their decks afforded such a scene as may be supposed after a sharp dispute, being promiscuously covered with carcasses, entrails and dismembered limbs. The main hatchway contained likewise several of their dead which had been thrown down during the action, though as I learnt afterwards they had been industriously employed in throwing the slain overboard since their first striking their colours to my coming on board. This ship was called Nuestra Señora de Cobadonga, commanded by Don Geronimo de Montero, a native of Portugal, whom in this service they term General. They had been 12 days from the island of Guam where they watered and refreshed and 72 from Acapulco, at which place they had sold their cargo from Manila, the returns of which amounted to about a million and a half dollars which they had on board, besides private money. At the time of engagement they had 32 guns ready for action, besides four 12 pounders which were mounted between decks but were not used, and eight that were in the hold; that all in all they had 44 guns on board. These were of different natures, from 12 to 6 pounders, amongst which were several brass guns of great length. Her gunnels quarters and tops contained 28 pedros, which went with chambers, and fired a 3 pound ball, besides the above-mentioned stones and nails, which villainous implements wounded several of our men. It was a long time before we could come to an estimation of the number of men. Their quarter bill which seemed regularly disposed amounted to 440 men, but we still had prisoners to 500. They likewise disagreed in the number of their dead, but the General assured me we could not have killed less than 50, adding that it was in vain to conceal their loss; but others insisted on 40. They had besides about 170 wounded, several which died a few days later. The General himself was wounded in the breast with a musket ball, and rendered incapable of being removed for some days. The Captain of the soldiers, who was nephew to the Viceroy of Mexico, was mortally wounded, and died a few hours after. The gunner was likewise too much wounded to be removed, but recovered afterwards. To sum up the whole, the ship was surprisingly shattered in her hull, masts and rigging; the mainmast was half shot through, and few of the shrouds left standing. The ship being shot through in this manner may serve to refute a ridiculous opinion which has been handed down amongst all seafaring people as a certain tradition, that the sides of the galleons were always built shot proof; but we found by experience that they were not strong enough to resist our grapeshot, much more our 24-pounder balls.

As to our ship, we received several shot on her hull. The foremast and bowsprit had likewise each a shot from the great guns, but not of consequence enough to disable either; but the barge and pinnace which were on the booms were much shattered, as was likewise one of the spare topmasts. As to the rigging, some of the fore shrouds and the fore jeers with several of the running ropes were shot. In the action one man was killed at his quarters, another died within an hour of his wounds; and a third after an amputation of his leg; and the 2nd Lieut. with fifteen men besides were wounded. Thus ended engagement, in which if the number of our guns and the weight of our metal be impartially considered, it must be confessed we engaged the enemy with great advantages on our side though on the other it may be objected that they were far superior to us in numbers, having as I observed before 550 men all well armed either with pedros, muskets or half-pikes, being likewise well provided with close quarters, having a strong network of two inch rope which laced over the waist and under which they fought their guns, their half pikes being chiefly designed to defend it and thrust through, and had besides a company of soldiers; whereas we mustered but 227, 27 of which were small boys.

It had been a short, bloody and costly engagement for the Spaniards in men and gold. In less than one hour and a half it was all over. The Spanish officers had acted bravely, but the stupidity of their governor who had filled them with false confidence had cost them the richest prize ever captured on the high seas. The governor of the Philippines now sought to excuse his defeat by stating to his king that the combat had been between vessels of unequal strength. The Centurion was a faster sailer, he said, more manoeuvrable. She had more guns and higher bulwarks that protected her men while the Cobadonga's gun ports were narrow and confining and did not allow for the same freedom of manoeuvre. All this was true. But they were not the reasons for the Spanish defeat. The British triumphed because they were resolute and determined to capture the prize. There was no friendly shore nearby for safety. In defeat the British could not expect the same treatment they had given to their prisoners. The Centurion's crew had also used an ingenious system of fire power. Since their guns were less than half-manned a crew of flying cannoneers ran from one gun to the other reloading and firing so that the firing against the enemy ship was continuous. Within a half mile range the Centurion's guns were able to inflict heavy damage. This coupled with a withering fire from Jacob Blackbeard's sharp-shooters on the yards decimated the enemy.

Saumarez was made captain of the galleon, which was immediately commissioned as a King's ship. His first job was to transfer the treasure and prisoners to the Centurion. Unfortunately, the weather suddenly turned stormy and for some days it was impossible to remove either. There were 492 prisoners and treasure to guard, and both ships were in need of repairs after the engagement. The only place the Commodore could return to under these conditions was the Canton River where he could hardly anticipate a joyful welcome from the Mandarins.

A letter from Anson with instructions for Saumarez about the crew of the Cobadonga

By Commodore George Anson Esq.
Commander in Chief of his Majesties Ships
designed on a particular expedition
Having appointed the Centurion Prize a ship in his Majesties Service and discharg'd the fifteen men being officers and seamen and the sixty prisoners herein after mentioned out of his Majesties ship Centurion into his Majesties ship the Centurion Prize.

You are hereby required and directed to bear the said officers and seamen as part of the ships complement ordering your pursor to victual them at whole allowance of all species of provisions and to bear the sixty prisoners as supernumeraries causing them to be victualled at two thirds allowance of all species of provisons for which this shall be your warrant given under my Hand on Board the Centurion at sea this 21st June 1743.

G Anson

To Captain Philip Saumarez
Commander of his Majesties ship Centurion Prize

June 22nd Cape Espiritu Santo distance 77 leagues. Lat 13° 12' N, Lon 238° 35' W. Aboard the Centurion Prize

The weather proved uncertain being subject to squalls and showers of rain. Were employed in sending away the money which besides what was in the passengers' and officers' chests was chiefly contained in small chests containing each 3,000 and others 4,000 dollars. At 10 made an easy sail with the Commodore to the N.E. til daylight, then brought to, his boat coming on board. At 9 AM. I hoisted the small launch out to assist in carrying the money on board the Commodore. At noon it was calm but the weather looked black and a great eastern swell began to rise. Within the 24 hours five of our prisoners died of wounds.

June 23rd 1743. Cape Espiritu Santo 26 leagues. Lat 13° 45' N, Lon 238° 35'W

The first part it began to blow fresh with dark lowering weather. A great eastern sea raising but continuing sending the money away, the ship keeping under way for the convenience of the boats laying alongside. Steering to the N.E. the wind at W.N.W. At 8 PM. we brought to to the northward; found it impracticable to hoist our boat there being too great a sea and we moored under the lee quarter, and the remainder of the 24 hours it blew very hard with much thunder lightning and rain. 6 AM. handed the topsails which were much shattered being cotton sails and lay to under bare poles. At 7 our pinnace being stove and alongside we cut her away. The ironwork the bobstay was secured to breaking, occasioned the bowsprit fetching much away. At noon were laying to near the Commander; discovered a large shot hole in the starboard counter between wind and water to which I ascribed the ship's making water but cannot at present examine it.

June 24th 1743. Cape Espiritu Santo distance 31 leagues. Lat 14° 29' N, Lon 237° 58' W

The first part hard gales with rain and a great sea, the middle part grew more moderate. The wind rounding about to the eastward of the south which the prisoners told us would bring fair weather. In the morning the weather was much more moderate. At 9 the Commander made the sign to make sail and stood to the N.E. the winds at S.E. We following him fixed a new bobstay. One of the prisoners died of his wounds. Found that the shot hole in the counter to go quite through; this we leaded over and caulked.

June 25th 1743. Cape Espiritu Santo distance 60 leagues. Lat 15° 25' N, Lon 239° 04' W

The first part fresh gales and the latter part moderate and fair. Continuing our course to the N.E. At 6 PM. brought to to the eastward. Our prisoners beginning to recover from the panic secured a 100 every night under hatches with sentries over them, having mustered them and found a 195 including the wounded. In the morning the Commander's boat came on board and we began to send the money away, but having lost the long boat in the last gale obliged us to hoist our great launch out. At 7 made an easy sail to the northward with a south east wind. The General being tolerably recovered was sent on board the Commander. Found a strong current setting to the northward.

*June 26th 1743. Cape Espiritu Santo 74 leagues. Lat 16° 16'
N, Lon 239° 05' W*

The 24 hours moderate and fair. Employed in sending
the money away; at 6 PM. sent a launch away loaded,
having to the value of 55,000 pounds sterling on board
her in chests of silver. Continuing our course to the
North West quarter; AM. swayed the fore topmast up
and set the foretopsail; employed in searching the hold
but began to find our money decrease considerably that
we were obliged to have recourse to the passengers'
chests where several parcels were found. From our first
beginning to ship off to this instant esteem by a general
calculation that I have sent on board 1,300,000 dollars,
besides some wrought plate. Two of our prisoners died
of their wounds.

*A letter from Saumarez to Anson (unrevised) in which he explains the
damage done to the Cobadonga after the engagement with the Centurion.*
Sir
*Pursuant to your orders I have heal'd the ship and made as strict a search
as was possible, yet the success has not answered my expectation having
discovered the impression but of three shot, two of them on the rounding of
the larboard bow, I judge the first to have been made by a 24 pound ball,
it had penetrated near 3 inches in the middle of the plank, and was about
2 foot under the water line, according to our present draught of water; and
in the time of engagement must have been near 5 foot; allowing for a
weather roll. The other was 3 foot abaft it, and somewhat higher, but had
not gone so far in. and I believe was a 9 pounder. Yet to neither of these
can any leaks be ascribed. However I ordered the first to be leaded over
and well caulked. In examining her abaft we found a shot hole in the
rudder which had gone quite through at the water's edge and likewise her*

sheathing in general appears much decayed and in several places is broken away, in which parts the butt heads were very open, the oakum being quite rotten. These we have likewise caulked and repaired but since writing the ship I find she makes as much water as before; the leak appearing constant which must be owing to some defect which I doubt it is not in our powers to remedy but by careening her in order to inspect the bottom thoroughly.

The difficulty of sailing the shattered Cobadonga through the squalls and large seas combined with the duty of guarding so many prisoners with so few men, prompted Saumarez to transfer the treasure to the Centurion as quickly as he could. There was little time to accurately count the gold and silver. That would have to be done later in the relative quiet of the Canton River. For the moment the task of both ships was to find a safe harbour on the China coast before the storms that preceded the monsoon season began.

By June 27 the weight of the treasure removed from the Cobadonga was so great that her upper deck guns had to be substituted for ballast to offset the tonnage of gold and silver transferred to the Centurion. Fortunately a following wind helped speed the boats north-west towards the China coast as Saumarez continued to find more bags of dollars and chests of gold and silver plate. But as the wind increased the prize kept falling behind the faster Centurion so that she was taken in tow on the evening of June 29. On this same day Saumarez received from the cutter his official commission as captain of the Centurion Prize signed by Anson, and as captain of a post ship he proudly hoisted the British colours and pendant. The officers and men of the newly appointed King's ship cheered and saluted the Commander with eleven guns which was returned by a firing of nine.

At last on June 30 at 6 pm the north-east of the island of Luconia was sighted. The weather turned fair with little wind and this gave Saumarez time to examine some of the chests that still lay in the hold of the prize. Many of them were found to contain false bottoms in which large quantities of unregistered gold was concealed.

Once the weather improved the remainder of the prisoners were transferred to the Centurion and put under strict guard. The Spanish Captain de Montero, who was not too seriously wounded, was kept in the Commodore's great cabin. Below the Commodore in Saumarez's former quarters, the 17 surviving Spanish officers were held. The remainder of the Spanish crew was held in a section of the Centurion's badly ventilated orlop. The weather was terribly hot and the Spaniards half suffocated in the steaming hold. The prisoners, who out-numbered the crew by more than two to one, were guarded day and night by armed sentries and threatened with death at the slightest disobedience. While there was great elation at the victory there was also anxiety at the large number of Spaniards in captivity and the temptation their treasure would hold for the enemy.

The monsoon season had arrived as the two ships sailed warily north past Luconia (Luzon) and the Babuyan Islands, then east by north to Macao. There were many navigational hazards to overcome. The area they were passing through was a maze of small islands and shoals, which they were discovering for the first time. Their reference to Dampier's unreliable charts only caused confusion. Only constant soundings and common sense helped to avoid the coral reefs and low lying islands. Progress was further complicated by strong currents running at over four knots.

July 2nd 1743. Cape Bajadore distance 167 leagues. Lat 20° 11' N, Lon 242° 39' W

The first and middle part moderate and fair, the wind at the north east; towards the latter the wind began to strengthen and round about to the westward; as we now esteem ourselves on the change of the monsoon grew apprehensive of the stormy weather. At 3 were taken in tow again. Saw several canoes passing from one island to the other but none came near us. In the evening some fires were made on shore. As to any anchoring places or bays we could discover none promised any security for ships unless they lay on the islands that formed the southern side of the straits and which we were a considerable distance from. Dampier relates that he rode there 50 days and was at last blown off by a hard southerly wind. At 6 AM. these islands [Lema Islands] still on sight bearing North East by East distance 12 leagues. Struck down four of the lower deck guns being 12 pounders.

July 5th 1743. Cape Bajadore distance 69 leagues. Lat 21° 26' N, Lon 244° 50' W

These 24 hours the wind veered back to the South East which brought us moderate weather which we improved to our utmost, crowding all our sails to arrive if possible to some port in China before the change of the moon, which is generally attended with tempestuous weather. The sun being almost in the zenith made it very difficult observing.

July 7th 1743. Cape Bajadore distance 136 leagues. Lat 22° 03′ N, Lon 248° 54′ W

The first part had some squalls with rain but the middle and latter part proved moderate and fair. At 2 PM. in one of the squalls the cable we towed by broke, but the Commander hoisted his boat out and took us in tow again. Sent on board several boys with bags of dollars with some wrought plate. At 7 AM. saw the land bearing West North West and it appeared like a small homock rising out of the horizon.

By July 9 the Grand Ladrone bore north-west 27 miles. At 3 pm a sail sighted on the horizon and bound in the direction of Canton was suspected of being a French warship and a general alarm was raised. Though no one had definite knowledge, some of the captured Spanish documents on the Cobadonga informed them that war with France was imminent. Any ship suspected of being French could mean an engagement. With the immense treasure carried in the hold the British sailors were extra sensitive to any armed foreign ships in the immediate vicinity. Now that the galleon's treasure was theirs the crew of the Centurion had no intention of giving it up without a fierce fight. As always their best defence seemed to be their aggressiveness.

Saumarez was ordered to send all his men except ten to reinforce the Commodore. In the evening all Spanish arms were thrown overboard, cabins nailed up and Saumarez was prepared to quit the prize if there was to be a battle. The Commodore's boat remained alongside the Cobadonga all night, ready to remove Saumarez and his ten men should the sail turn out to be a French man-of-war. In the morning the ship was seen less than five miles off. She hoisted French colours and Anson and Saumarez showed theirs and gave chase. But the Frenchman crowded away under full sail and eluded them. However, at ten that evening the British ships caught up with the Frenchman and the Centurion fired two guns at her which missed, mainly due to the distance. The ship escaped, but since both were sailing towards the Canton River it seemed only a matter of time before they should meet again.

When they arrived at Macao on July 11, one of Anson's first acts was to send ashore some of his prisoners. They demanded such constant attention that their presence constituted a hazard. As soon as arrangements could be made the remaining prisoners would be sent away. The Spaniards who remained aboard were still confined to the steaming orlop below deck.

Impatient to move with his treasure to a protected anchorage the Commodore decided he would not await the uncertain permission of the Hoppo to sail into the Canton River as far as the Bocca Tigris. Instead a Chinese pilot was hired, and on July 14 the Centurion and her prize proceeded the forty miles up river to the new anchorage. Off the entrance of the passage into the Bocca Tigris stood two old Chinese forts, each mounting ten small iron cannons. They would be no match for the Centurion's superior fire power and remained manned but silent as the man-of-war dropped anchor nearby.

Anson was in no mood to be further victimised by Chinese chicanery or to be at the mercy of bribing Frenchmen or Spaniards who, he knew, would do everything to frustrate the provisioning of his ship for the voyage home. Also, it would not be long before the word spread of the vast treasure they had in their hold. Their safety depended on their own strength and vigilance.

The Commodore had no doubt that his return with the prize would send a tremor of fear through the Chinese that would be felt all the way to the Imperial Palace at Peking. But he was uncertain of the effect of his visit upon the East India merchantmen whose help he might need. As expected, it was not very long before the Mandarin in command of one of the forts came alongside in a great state of agitation to demand what two ships were doing in the Bocca Tigris without a permit. Saumarez had hired an interpreter at Macao who informed the Mandarin, in case it was not clear, that the Centurion was a man-of-war belonging to the King of England. She should be well known by now on the Canton. But this particular Hoppo knew nothing of the rights of ships of His Majesty's Navy. He was told that the Centurion carried 60 large guns, 400 muskets and 400 barrels of powder and her prize was also armed. She intended to proceed further up the Canton River seeking safe shelter until the typhoon season was over, when, watered and victualled, she would sail home for England.

The Mandarin was convinced that in spite of what the Commodore said about being a representative of the English King, really he was nothing more than a 'ladrone' — a thief. Why else would this ship carry, as the Mandarin had already heard, so much treasure aboard. The Chinese Mandarins in this part of the river were to call all the crew 'ladrones' and the Commodore himself was known as the 'Great Ladrone'. Two customs men were then put aboard but Anson assured the Mandarin that they would pay no harbour dues. Although the customs men remained to make certain the Centurion was not a trading vessel they were not allowed to measure the ship and remained only as guests.

July 15th 1743. Were sailing through the Bogue of Tigres
These 24 hours moderate and fair. At ½ past 1 PM. having drove clear of the Commodore came to in 7

fathoms with the sheet anchor, this being the only one we can trust to. At 3 PM. weighed per signal; falling calm were obliged to come to again. In the evening swayed up the foretopmast and at 6 AM. got the mainmast up. At 10 weighed per signal and sailed through the Bogue with the wind at the West South West. The Commodore sent the 18 oared boat with our officer to Canton to solicit the Viceroy for permission to anchor in the River near Whampoa.

July 16th 1743. Were getting under sail being 7 miles above the Bogue
The whole part uncertain weather with squalls of rain. At 3 PM. a squall coming on from the westward came to per signal in 5 fathoms. At 6 AM. discerned two ships coming up with French colours on which the Commodore cleared ship and sent for most of our hands to reinforce him. I received orders at the same time to prepare on board with the rest of the people in case he engaged. At 11 received orders to weigh and keep ahead of the Commander who got under sail. At ½ past the two ships came up with us, one of which wore a pendant. They were about the bigness of our India ships and seemed to have no lower tier or ports but effected an air of being prepared to engage us in case we had molested them. The Commander sent his boat on board for news but could gather nothing material besides war continuing with Spain, but with no other Prince; all this time I was employed in purchasing my anchor.

Since both the captain of the French India merchantman and the Commodore had no fresh information as to whether war had actually been declared it was decided in the interest of both that they would not fight one another. Thus having established mutually this principle of nonaggression each ship went about her business free of interference. In this fashion an uneasy peace was declared between the two nations on the Canton River.

July 17th 1743. Anchored in the Bogue

At 2 PM. we anchored near the Commander in 6 ½ fathoms a little below the 3rd bar; a pagoda bearing North West 4 or 5 miles and the entrance of the Bogue South South East 4 or 5 leagues. At 5 moored per signal. The two French ships having run considerable above us anchored, on which the remainder of the hands were sent back to me. At 6 AM. one of our India ships arrived here and anchored and saluted the Commander with 21 guns. He returned 19. This ship had been 20 months from England and came last from Bombay. She anchored near us at the Commodore's request, who imagined stopping our India ships from going up would facilitate our obtaining leave to go to Wampo and accordingly gave out that unless we went up we should suffer none of our ships to trade with them which did us considerable service. At 8 our boat returned from Canton but without success there having been a mistake in the report. The forts at the Bogue considered us as India ships; both the European and Chinese merchants were so extremely sly and afraid of bringing themselves into trouble that they would scarce be seen conversing with the officers nor would any of the Mandarins receive the letter for the Viceroy but said one of them would be sent to enquire into matters.

Aboard the Cobadonga Saumarez was continually finding more treasure hidden in false ceilings and secreted behind panels. On one occasion a suspiciously heavy load of cheeses that were sliced open was found to contain solid gold bullion. To date 1,278,546 Spanish gold and silver dollars and thousands of pounds in weight of beautifully wrought silver and gold had been discovered. In those days the value according to Saumarez amounted to £313,121 15 shillings and 7 ½ pence. But there is evidence now that he grossly understated. Each piece of magnificently wrought filigree silver today would be priceless. In addition, the Centurion carried the treasure of Payta and the other Spanish prizes which altogether amounted to over £500,000 in 1743. This excluded jewels and thousands of gold, silver and jade ornaments as well as tapestries, damasks and rare spices.

Second Lieutenant Denis was sent up to Canton with a number of Spanish prisoners to deliver a letter on behalf of the Commodore to the palace of the Chantuk. The 18-oared boat upon arrival at Canton received a polite reception from the Mandarins. Denis requested a chop or order for daily provisions and for sea stores for the voyage home. The visitors were willing to pay well for their supplies. The Mandarins at the court of the Viceroy closely questioned both Denis and the Spanish prisoners, some of whom he brought with him. Why, the Mandarins asked, did the English not chop off the heads of their prisoners as was customary in war. The prisoners replied that this was not the normal practice among these people. Indeed, they had been treated with unusual civility. Later the captain of the Cobadonga wrote to Saumarez thanking him for his many kindnesses and regretted that it was doubtful he would ever have the opportunity of reciprocating.

The minds of the Mandarins were confused by the ruthlessness and strength of the British in battle and the excessive politeness shown to their conquered who were neither made vassals nor beheaded. The Viceroy was an astute man and realised that not only was he dealing with some unusual people, but also that they were powerful and very rich with treasure. Immediately, his attitude changed. He was not treating with lawless pirates as he had been led to believe, but with disciplined soldiers serving under 'The Grand King Captain' on the 'Grand King Ship'. A message was sent to the Imperial Emperor at Peking suggesting a new approach to the Commodore and his requests.

Anson, however, did not wish to rely exclusively on the good will of the Chinese. He had already prevailed upon the East Indiamen in the Bocca Tigris not to carry on any more trade until such time as the Centurion and her prize were officially allowed to go further down the river to anchor at Whampoa. The East Indiamen cooperated and decided to stand fast behind the Commodore. The desired effect was soon realised.

July 20th 1743. Anchored below the bars in the Canton River
Close, covered weather generally. About 4 in the afternoon the sky looked very black to the northward over the land with much thunder and lightning, but dispelled without reaching us. This morning the Commodore was visited by two principal Mandarins which were attended by several boats; the design was to know what the Commodore wanted and to endeavour to prevail with us to let the India ships go up and at the same time persuade us to remain where we were; but finding all the arguments proved ineffectual they promised to represent the account we had given of

ourselves and what we wanted to the Vice-Roy, (as he is here called the Chantuk), and to give us a final answer in 5 days in which time they desired we would forebear sending our boats to Canton, which was promised.

July 27th 1743. Sailing up the Canton River. The Pagoda bore West 3 miles distance

Most part calm. In the morning the linguist which was employed by the Mandarins brought the Commodore his chop or permission to sail higher up the river, but not so far as Wampo where the European ships lay. We were not to hire any Hongs or factories at Canton or build any banghazars ashore and we were promised to be supplied with what refreshments we wanted during our stay here and with what provisions were necessary to enable us to pursue our voyage to England; it being one of the considerations we agreed to, that we were to sail on the first of the northern monsoons. Our getting this permission was a matter of great surprise to all the Europeans, the French and the Portuguese particularly, who with the Chinese merchants did us all the ill offices that lay in their power. The article of the mensuration of our ships being a difficulty it was never imagined we should have surmounted, and which as King's ships the Commodore was resolved that at all events should never be submitted to. At 6 AM. unmoored per signal. 9 weighed, the Indiamen sailing up with us; kept the boats ahead it falling calm. The soundings I observed to be irregular for the first 5 or 6 miles having from 5 ½ to 4 fathoms; and we drove over a spot where we sounded twice at 19 fathoms of water. The channel did not seem to be above a cable and a half broad, but was soft mud.

July 28th 1743. Sailing up the Canton River

These 24 hours calm and sultry. At 5 PM. the ebb tide coming down strong. Anchored per signal in 7 fathoms having drove up in all about 10 or 11 miles; having obtained leave from the Vice-Roy for our prisoners to be sent to Macao. Several Chinese boats arrived from Canton which in the morning were sent away with all the Spanish men excepting 80 of the latter which we reserved in this ship and 15 the Commodore detained aboard him. Found that in mustering them we had lost 12 since our first passing the Bogue which we believed escaped in some of the small boats that sold refreshments. At 10 AM. weighed per signal, the wind blowing down river drove us with our head sails to the mast.

July 29th 1743. Moored in the Canton River. A small Hoppo house in a cluster of trees SBE ½ mile and Wampo Point NWBW ½ W 4 miles

24 hours moderate and fair, the weather much cooler than usual. 4 PM. anchored per signal in 8 fathoms with the small bower not designing to proceed any further up being within 5 or 6 miles of Wampo; but the India ship proceeded up. At 5 moored and made the signal, converting the India ships anchor for a best bower; discharged the pilot. This place was commodiously situated for our wintering here and was more convenient than if we had been at Wampo where laying amongst so many different European ships would naturally have bred distractions and animosities amongst the people. The river here was about 1 ¾ miles broad

each side being a low paddy ground where they sow rice and had the prospect of several pretty villages, but the Chinese would not permit us to recreate ourselves there under pretence that we might be insulted by the natives; had several of their men-of-war boats on either side of the river to guard and take care of us as they told us; during the ebb tide we used to fill our casks and jars; the water when suffered to subside became clear and perfectly sweet.

Letter from General Don Jeronimo Montero to Captain Philip Saumarez thanking him for his courteous treatment of the Spanish officers and crew taken prisoner. Macao August 30th 1743.

Dear Sir,

On the occasion of touching at that port, the bearer of this, who is Don Juan, will explain to you the extent of my estimation. I must write to you only to give you due appreciation for the great zeal you have shown in favouring the persons who are prisoners in this ship, for all say and declare in this City of Macao that they have received from you a special regard and affection and that they have nothing with which to make a return. And this being a circumstance which puts me at such an obligation, I wish to inform you, that, being assured that I desire to serve you, you give me great reason to show my gratitude under conditions which prevent me from doing so.

I, thank God, have recovered from my pains, although there still remains those in my feet, but by walking I hope to get better soon, in a few days from now, if I am so fortunate, I hope to see you in port, where we shall be able to speak more at our ease. And meanwhile, I pray God guard your life many years.

I beg to remain with respect and affection.

Jeronimo Montero

Captain Philip Saumarez
Senor Don Philipe Saumarez (God keep him many years)

During August and September small quantities of supplies came aboard the Centurion and her prize. But none of the food was in sufficient amount to prepare the ships for the voyage home. Every now and then Saumarez would turn up another cache of silver plate or gold which he would send onto the Centurion. Barrels of gunpowder were dried, rigging respliced or replaced and the carpenters repaired the masts and hull where Spanish shot had entered during their engagement with the Cobadonga. On August 10 Saumarez sent seventy empty powder boxes aboard the Centurion in which some of the loose money could be stored. Captured arrack at the rate of half a pint per man a day was served to the sailors. Inferior Chinese samsho was allocated to the prisoners at one pint for every three men. The heavy drinking crew, who appeared to have endless capacity for alcohol, were seldom disciplined for drunkeness. They seemed to be able to hold their liquor. Hundreds of small tasks kept the crew constantly busy, but both officers and men were impatient to leave China. The subtle harassment of the Mandarins combined with the numerous small difficulties placed in the way of the English at every request created an uneasy atmosphere.

The supply of provisions still remained on a limited basis in spite of all promises. This was highly unsatisfactory. For the voyage to England the Centurion required huge quantities of food which the Chinese showed no willingness to sell. Also, there was the question of harbour dues which the Chinese continued to insist upon. These two matters had to be settled before the Centurion could sail out of Chinese waters. One as a matter of principle, the other as a matter of necessity.

The English supercargoes could find no satisfactory solution. There were a number of issues they too wished to resolve, and the presence of the Centurion gave them additional strength. Indeed their attitude was much different from the English merchantmen whom Saumarez had met on the previous spring. The East Indiamen he now dealt with knew their own fate would hang upon Anson's negotiations with the Chantuk whom they could never hope to meet. But they still waited for an answer to the Commodore's letter delivered to the Chantuk by Denis. Rather than wait any longer for a reply Anson and Saumarez decided to press personally for an interview with the Viceroy at Canton.

With a retinue of forty sailors dressed in brilliantly coloured uniforms of scarlet and blue, silver buckles on their shoes, wearing large three-cornered hats, and attended by all the supercargoes, Anson and Saumarez headed for Canton. Minute instructions were left to the commanders of the ships what course of action was to be followed if they were taken prisoner or killed. At all costs the treasure had to be saved, the Cobadonga burned, and the Centurion to sail out of the river and await further orders in Macao Roads.

October 13th 1743. Moored in our former anchoring place in Canton Riper about 2 miles below the Wampo Point
Continuing squally with rain. I received orders from the Commodore to attend him up the Canton. Accordingly at 3 PM. he went up in his barge attended by most of the supercargoes of the European ships in the boats. His design being to wait on the Vice-Roy to solicit him for necessaries for the ships. At his going from hence he was saluted by both ships, and as he rowed by the European ships at Wampo they all saluted him excepting the three French ships. Were supplied with 10

fathoms of rope and with nails to would the fish on the main mast with.

As the procession rowed off to Canton, at the last moment there were vigorous remonstrations from the local Mandarins that it was useless to go. But this protest influenced no one. Upon arrival in the city the Commodore's party was given accommodation in the East India Company's premises alongside the Canton River.

In 1743, Canton contained one million inhabitants who lived in derelict shacks outside the Great Wall or in somewhat better accommodation within the protected precinct of the city. Inside the Great Wall was the Chantuk's sumptuous residence or Yamen. It was set in the centre of magnificent green parks amidst flowering jasmin trees, and tame deer roamed freely through the grounds. Along Canton's river bank were the many warehouses of the English, Dutch, French, Swedish and Norwegian traders as well as the large hongs or Chinese depots. Where the river was unoccupied by either warehouses or offices thousands of junks lay alongside the banks as floating homes for the swarming population.

The Commodore's party settled down to wait in the English quarter for the interview with the Chantuk. During this period the English East India merchants ordered the sea-going provisions for which Anson paid 800 dollars in advance. These provisions were stored in a warehouse waiting for the chop from the Chantuk before they could be delivered aboard the Centurion.

The delays at Canton were interminable. One excuse after another was offered by the Mandarins for their inability to arrange the meeting with the Viceroy. Behind these excuses lay the influence of the French who did everything in their power to prevent it. It is entirely conceivable that no meeting would have taken place had it not been for an accident which radically changed the attitude of the Hoppos.

Lieutenant August van Keppel, who had been sent to Canton on the Commodore's orders on November 30, 1743, reported from Whampoa where he was aboard the Centurion 'we hear there is a great fire at Canton that has burned down the Swedes and Danes factory and many other valuable ones as well.' The fire raging in Canton had spread through the wooden shacks of the city and was threatening to engulf the centre of Canton itself. The flames had already devoured many of the large, valuable hongs.

The Chinese were incapable, it seemed, of organising a proper brigade to systematically contain the conflagration. They had neither a fire fighting force nor an organised militia. The intervention of forty British sailors who ruthlessly tore down the rickety shacks that were in the path of the fire is said to have stopped the flames from spreading and destroying the city. When the fire was out the Mandarins personally expressed their gratitude to the Commodore for his services. The following day permission for the interview with the Chantuk at his royal palace was granted.

The atmosphere of the meeting between the Commodore and the Viceroy was regal. The Commodore was carried to the palace in a canopied chair adorned with gold and silver satins by sixteen uniformed coolies. Next to him was his second-in-command, Saumarez, and following them was Lieutenant the Honourable August van Keppel, aged seventeen, and all the captains of all the East India Company's vessels, both English and foreign. Forty sailors of the Centurion in their gaudy uniforms brought up the rear of the long procession.

A Chinese guard sent by the Chantuk met the procession and escorted it through the winding congested streets to the grounds of the Yaman. Here ten thousand troops were drawn up carrying colourful pendants, maces and pikes and forming a human aisle through which the procession passed into the Great Hall of Audience where the Chantuk was seated under a magnificent silken canopy surrounded on either side by his Chief Mandarins. Anson, to expedite the negotiations brought with him a Mr Flint, an able interpreter from the East India Company who was born in China and spoke the language fluently. The Chantuk beckoned to a servant who brought a chair which was placed beside the Viceroy for the Commodore, who unlike the rest of his retinue, did not remove his hat, and alone was allowed to sit down. This was a meeting between the two representatives of equal rank.

The Viceroy was exceedingly curious. This was his very first contact with a white man and he was anxious to observe this particular breed who had come to Canton not to trade but to ask without fear of favour for provisions. The Chantuk had never heard of a white man of rank who was contemptuous of commerce and yet who amassed, it was reputed, enormous wealth in his King's name by capturing at will treasure ships of his enemies. He did not kill his enemies, as was his right, but treated them more like friends. This was very confusing. Furthermore, this King's representative would not obey the rules of his country by paying harbour dues. His great ship with the immense guns was ready to dispute this contention.

Contrary to what was anticipated the Viceroy showed understanding. He listened to all the minor complaints of the East Indiamen and agreed to rectify them. Without hesitation he consented to victual the Centurion and her prize for their long voyage home. In Anson's presence he gave orders to the

Mandarins in charge to immediately grant the required chop. The issue of payment of harbour dues was not brought up, neither by the Chantuk nor by Anson. In this way neither lost face and a precedent of non-payment for men-of-war was tacitly established. Shortly afterwards the Viceroy and the Commodore exchanged polite farewells and the British processions took their leave, saluted by three Chinese guns as was customary. The following day Anson and Saumarez were back aboard their ship taking on provisions for the long passage to England.

Cobadonga had becomes a liability. She constantly took in water from her battle damage, and most of the rigging was in need of replacement. Her pumps were decayed and the crew bailed constantly by hand. All her heavy guns had been transferred to the Centurion to keep her floating above the water line.

The English supercargoes came on board the Centurion on December 4 to say goodbye and thank the Commodore for his help. The presence of the Royal Navy had done much to secure the British position on the Canton River. After saluting the British East Indiamen with nine guns they made preparations to depart. Large quantities of sea stores had been put aboard by hundreds of Chinese coolies so that by December 7 the Centurion and her prize were ready to set sail out of the river. Saumarez had great difficulty manoeuvring the Cobadonga. The waterlogged hull became uncontrollable and drove through a row of piles on the river bank, but was finally brought under command. On December 10 the Centurion's boats had to tow the Cobadonga over the last bar so she could sail free. Finally, on the following morning Saumarez was able to bring his ship safely through the Bogue of Tigris and anchor.

Next day at high water the Centurion and Cobadonga slowly made their way out past the forts of the Bocca Tigris to where the Canton River joined the roadstead to Macao. The East India ships in the vicinity boomed their respect with salvos of twenty-one gun salutes. At Macao orders were given for all the remaining Spanish prisoners to be put ashore in junks as had been arranged with the Mandarins, with only a few dozen Indians, Lascars and black men retained as crew.

In late December Captain Saumarez sadly took down the colours from the masthead of his ship. A few days earlier his officers had handed him a petition which he passed on to the Commodore. The Centurion Prize was in no condition to undertake the voyage home. Neither Saumarez nor the Commodore could disagree with the findings. Therefore the Cobadonga would be sold. At last when he was given the command he always wanted there was no ship to captain. The irony was made more cruel when Saumarez was forced to join the other supernumeraries since he had already relinquished his post aboard the Centurion to Lieutenant Denis.

Although the Cobadonga had turned out to be as unseaworthy as most of the Spanish prizes that they had captured, it was made known through Portuguese agents that the Spaniards would be glad to have the ship returned, whatever her condition. All useful supplies were transferred to the Centurion. Then a Portuguese delegation mysteriously appeared to negotiate the sale. A sum of 6,000 dollars was paid by certain Portuguese citizens of Macao who agreed also to be responsible for the prisoners. It was a trifling sum for so great a ship which still could be repaired given time and materials.

December 15th 1743. Anchored Macao Road
Favourable moderate weather which proved very fortunate for us as all our cables were very indifferent. A

gale of wind would infallibly have drove the ship either ashore or to sea. If the latter should occur we would have run more danger of foundering as the ship was very leaky and her upper works very open. Continuing sending away provisions of stores formerly received from the Centurion. Sent away also the following; cotton sails being half worn, one foresail, one main topsail, and an old sprit sail, two amplitude compasses and 8, ½ and ¼ minute glasses, with points, gaskets and all. In the morning I received an order from the Commander to deliver the ship to certain Portuguese inhabitants of Macao with all her appurtenances and what part of her cargo was on board on condition that they likewise received the prisoners we left on her. The Governor of the town on the Commander applying to him had refused admitting them in his garrison. These Portuguese on the rumour of the Prize's being designed to be burnt had offered to purchase her and obtained her for a sum of 6000 dollars having agreed to charge themselves with the prisoners. 20 of the unmarried prisoners were sent on board the Centurion as reinforcements to the ship's company. About noon Mr. Nutt, 3rd Lieutenant of the Centurion came on board with the above mentioned Portuguese and certified that the ship was to be delivered up to them. Accordingly, having taken away the colours I embarked with my officers and people and quitting the ship repaired on board the Centurion who weighed anchor and was laying to waiting for our arrival, bound for England.

The voyage home around the Cape of Good Hope was uneventful. The crew had remained in good health since they left Tinian and no more cases of scurvy were reported. On June 10, after a six month sea voyage, they entered the English Channel where they met an English privateer who informed them there had been war with France since March. As the Centurion sailed on a thick fog luckily descended and with her treasure she coasted unseen through the midst of the French fleet. At 10 am on June 15, 1744 the Centurion anchored at St Helens on the Isle of Wight where she began the voyage with her full squadron three years and nine months before.

CHAPTER FOURTEEN: THE RETURN

Few expeditions captured the imagination and admiration of the English people as did the voyage of the Centurion. Perhaps it was because no battle had yet been won against the French with whom they were now at war. Or no battle yet fought against the Spanish in Europe with whom they had been ostensibly at war for almost five years. But courage was admired. The survivors had surmounted the greatest obstacles and returned.

Before the return, news had filtered back from China of a great treasure captured from the Manila galleon. This intelligence swelled the welcome that awaited the crew at Portsmouth and the tumultuous reception they received in the streets of London. In the excitement the lost ships and men were forgotten: only the survivors counted.

The exploits of the survivors were gloriously feted at banquets. Contemporary journals like the *Gentleman's Magazine* publicised their triumphs with pride. The Navy basked in the reflected prestige. Stories of the great treasure grew as the crowds along the streets saw thirty two wagon loads of chests carried all the way from Portsmouth to the Tower of London for safekeeping. Although the reports of the exact sum varied, the cash value in England was considered at the time to be in excess of £800,000. Translating the bullion, gold and silver into present day terms it would be enormous — perhaps as much as £50,000,000. Since the entire budget of the Royal Navy in 1745 was only £2,813,586 one begins to realise the size of the cache. No greater prize has ever been captured by anyone before or since. The fortunes of the officers of the Centurion were assured. The commander-in-chief received an eighth of all prizes and the captain two eighths. This meant Anson's share was three-eighths of the total. Marine captains, sea lieutenants and masters took one eighth. One eighth went to Marine lieutenants, boatswains, gunners, pursers, carpenters, masters' mates, surgeons and chaplains, and one eighth to midshipmen, gunners' mates and quartermasters. Two eighths was divided among the able and ordinary seamen, volunteers, marines, cooks' mates and coopers. Everyone received some part of the wealth.

However, a squalid legal struggle took place as to what officers were entitled to the money. Supernumeraries by law were not eligible for prize money from the Manila galleon since they were not an official part of the complement of the Centurion. Morally, the supernumeraries had an indisputable claim. They had fought in the engagement. All had been survivors together, all had endured together and suffered together. In the end the gold destroyed close friendships.

The supernumeraries, in the legal struggles that followed, said they acted as officers and had taken a decisive part in the engagement with the treasure ship. The High Court of the Admiralty found for them. On appeal to the Lords the supernumeraries lost. This gave them entitlement only to seamen's shares. It was a notably unjust decision. Saumarez was deeply disturbed by the whole affair. 'This fatal law suit lays me under, and all my friends by restraining and preventing my assisting them in the manner I could wish is a most scandalous thing. And was I in the room of that prudentially scheming jesuitical person who first involved us in it, I should be most miserable being alive and ashamed to show my head.'

It was a disgraceful affair and ironically it was the testimony of Anson himself that lost the case for the supernumeraries. In a letter to his father in February 1746 Philip Saumarez finds the lawsuit so distasteful that he resolves as soon as possible to go to sea and if he should capture more prizes he will 'keep the lawyers clutches out'. The lawsuit was very expensive and it cast over the survivors a shadow of envy and jealousy that hardly deserved a place in so brave a venture. As one of the supernumeraries said, 'we had more terrible engagements in the courts of law than we ever had on the high seas.'

George Anson 'the father of the Royal Navy' and Charles Saunders were made First Lords of the Admiralty. Philip Saumarez was perhaps the most capable and talented of them all. In 1746 he was given his own command in the Nottingham and captured the Mars, one of the most prized French men-of-war, off Cape Clear. It was a notable victory. In 1747, when he was cut down by a French cannonball at the age of 34, he left a brilliant naval career unfulfilled. The will he left was as meticulous in detail as his logs, and his bequests forgot no one. To his friend and commander George Anson he left an emerald mourning ring to remember him by. Saumarez had realised the prophetic destiny that had haunted him throughout his career.

Letter to John de Saumarez Esq.

November 3rd 1747

Dear Brother, It is with the greatest concern I write this, to acquaint you of the death of your Brother Captain Philip Saumarez, who was slain in late action against eight of the enemy, six of which we have taken, the two others having escaped in the Night; The character he has left behind will always be a great honor to his memory — he is not only in loss to his relations, but likewise to his King and Country.

I have his corpse on board of me, the which is embalmed; next Friday is fixed for his Funeral, the which I do assure you will be performed with all military honors. Than him no Officer ever deserved it more; I cannot write to your father on this melancholy subject, but leave it to your prudence, to do so, as you shall judge proper.

I send you enclosed a copy of his will, and likwise a copy of what is in his Scrutoire, which I thought was most material, the originals have been put into it again. The Surgeons who embalmed the Corpse, tell me that if your poor brother had survived this, he could not have lived above a year longer, his lungs being grown to his side, and much wasted.

I have by me his Will, Watch, and a pair of gold buttons, and 46 Guineas, the whole delivered me by Mr Logie first Lieutenant of the Nottingham. As to all the rest of his things, Furniture, Plate and Clothes, I have them in my Ship the Keys of which are sealed in the Scrutoire.

I believe it will be sometime before I can see you, as I shall go to sea before you come over, it is necessary you should; I will tell them to put everything in charge of Mr Morhead.

I will once more request that I wish you to come over, and from hence you should go to London; I hope you will not think of any house to live at but my own, the which I do assure you will give me great pleasure.

Young Sauvaine is well, and still on board of the Nottingham, but shall go on board another ship. He seems a very promising youth, and I shall always be glad to serve him, to the utmost of my power.

Poor Nicholas my servant was killed in the action, I have taken his brother Peter with me. Pray remember my duty to my father and Mother, the usual compliments to my relations and friends.

I am dear Brother, yours affectionately

(signed) Philip Durell
[Saumarez brother-in-law]

GLOSSARY

AMPLITUDE: A bearing taken on a heavenly body, such as the sun, usually at sunset, to check the error in the compass. An azimuth.

BANGHAZAR: A large Chinese hut; used as storage for the Centurion's supplies while she was on the Canton River.

BRAIL: To secure a sail by drawing it in to its spar or stay by means of lines.

BARRICOE: Small Spanish sailing craft.

BRIG: A two-masted sailing ship square-rigged on both masts.

BRIGANTINE: A two-masted sailing ship square-rigged on the fore mast.

CADEY: Chinese weight.

CANDARINE: Chinese weight.

CAREEN: To beach and heel over a vessel, to gain access to the bottom for repairs, examination, cleaning etc.

CHACE: Corruption of 'chase', which was the chase of another craft.

CUTTER: Small boat kept aboard a larger ship. Could be rowed or sailed.

DEADEYE: A round wooden block without sheaves, but with three holes through it. It was secured to the lower ends of the shrouds (lateral stays bracing the masts) and flexible rope lanyards passed through the holes to opposing deadeyes on the chainplates. Slack rigging could be tightened by adjusting the lanyards, which had to be done periodically.

FATHOM: Measure of the depth of water. One fathom is six feet.

FISH: To make a temporary repair to a broken or sprung

(cracked) spar, by splinting it with shorter pieces of wood around the break and lashing them tightly round with rope. The repair was called a 'fish'.

GAMMONING: The rope lashings or ironwork which holds a bowsprit down on the bows. They take great strain.

GOLD DOLLAR: Spanish coin in use in the Americas in the 18th century.

GRAVE AND SHEATH: To clean off a ship's bottom and then cover it with copper sheet.

HALF PIKE: An axe-like weapon used in boarding or repelling boarders and issued to the crew on such occasions.

JACK: A flag. Also a flagstaff placed in the bows or on the bowsprit.

JESUIT'S BARD: Spanish sailing vessel.

JURY RIG: To arrange a makeshift (jury) rig after the loss of spars, rudder, rigging or canvas.

KNEES: Strong brackets bracing and linking the timbers of a wooden vessel.

LEAGUE: Three nautical miles (about 3 ½ land miles).

LEE QUARTER: After part of the vessel, on the side opposite the direction of the wind.

LUFF: To come up into the wind, usually in order to change direction or to impede movement by bringing the vessel into the eye of the wind.

MACE: Form of Chinese measure. Also a valued eastern spice.

NEW STOPPERED: Recently plugged or stopped (leak or seam); also refers to a temporary joining of the broken ends of rigging.

OAKUM: Soft material used to caulk the seams of a vessel, made from the fibres of old rope.

ORLOP: The lowest deck of a ship, used for stores, sick bay, prisoners etc; poorly lit and ventilated.

OUTRIGGER: A native sailing craft of the Pacific which has a pontoon secured to the main hull by struts. The pontoon and struts are the outrigger.

PAGODA: Chinese shrine, frequently a large outstanding building. PEDROS Small Spanish cannon.

PEKULL: Chinese measure.

PINNACE: Small boat kept aboard a larger ship. May be sailed or rowed. Also a small two-masted vessel with sails and oars.

PROA: Lightly built Pacific canoe capable of high speeds, with an outrigger on one side only.

RATTAN: Cane used by petty officers aboard men-of-war to enforce discipline.

REEVE: To run a rope through a block.

REEVE: A rope running through a block to obtain a purchase for either lifting or hauling in sails.

REEF: To reduce sail area in strong winds. The canvas is partially lashed to its spar with short ties.

SAMSHO: A cheap Chinese liquor.

SCORBUTICK: Pertaining to scurvy. Anti-scorbutics are scurvy-preventing food or drink, containing vitamin C.

SCUTTLE: To deliberately sink a vessel by admitting water through the hull.

SEROONS: Form of silver weight.

SHEAVES: The rollers in a block or pulley.

SHADDOCK A herb which was discovered on the Island of Juan Fernandez.

SNOW A brig (qv) with a short trysail mast aft of the lower main mast. SPANISH DOLLAR: Similar to a gold dollar and common in South America in the 18th century.

SPRITSAIL: Small sail attached to a yard on the bowsprit.

SLINGS: Part of the yardarm fittings, which supported the yard while allowing it to pivot.

SWAY: To join two parts of the same rope, usually to create a small loop or eye. To hoist or set up.

TACK: To change sailing direction by turning the ship's head through the eye of the wind.

TAKELLS: Form of Chinese weight.

VICTUALLER: Supply ship.

WESTINGS AND EASTINGS: Distance travelled in longitude to the west or east.

WEAR SHIP: To turn a ship in a controlled manner. Instead of gybing (swinging the stern through the wind) from one course to another, the ship's head is turned up into the wind and then round onto the new course off the wind.

SELECTED BIBLIOGRAPHY

Anson's reports to the Admiralty.

Bulkeley and Cummins: *A Voyage to the South Seas 1740.-1741.* First edition London 1734. Harrap 1927.

Byron, John: *A Narrative Containing an Account of the Great Distresses Suffered by Himself and his Companions on the Coast of Patagonia, 1740.-1746, and the Loss of the Wager Man-of-War.* 1768.

Dougan, Robert Ov. and A L Rouse: *Francis Drake 1628 and the Relation of a Wonderful Voyage* by William Cornelius Schouten 1619. World Publishing Company 1966.

Fletcher, Master Francis: *Sir Francis Drake, The World Encompassed.* Carefully collected out of the notes of Master Francis Fletcher, preacher. London 1628.

Hakluyt, Richard: *The Principal Navigations, Voyages, Traffiques and Discoveries of the English Nation.* Volume I. Reprint E. P. Dutton 1927.

Masefield, John: *Sea Life in Nelson's Time.* Sphere Books 1972.

Murray, Arthur (Viscount Elibank): *An Episode in the Spanish War 1739-1744.*

Pack, S W C: *The Wager Mutiny,* London 1964.

Shelton, R A: *Captain James Cook after Two Hundred Years.* The British Museum 1969.

Shelvocke, Captain G: *A Voyage Around the World.* Cassell 1928.

Somerville, Vice Admiral Boyle: *Commodore Anson's Voyage into the South Seas and Around the World.* Wm Heinemann 1934.

Walter, Reverend Richard: *Anson's Voyage Around the World 1740.-1744.* London 1747.

Williams, Glyndur: *Documents Relating to Anson's Voyage Around the World 1740-1744.* Navy Records Society 1967.

Young, John: *An Affecting Narrative of the Unfortunate Voyage and Catastrophe of HMS Wager, one of Commodore Anson's Squadron in the South Seas Expedition.* London 1751.

Saumarez, Philip: A personal handwritten biography of Captain Philip Saumarez, written by a member of the family in the nineteenth century.

Saumarez, Philip: An abstract of a Journal, 7 December 1742. Macao.

Saumarez, Philip: A collection of letters, notes and observations written between 1736 and 1746 on the circumnavigation of the Centurion and aspects of navy life.

Saumarez, Philip: The log of the Centurion 1739-1744.

All letters by Josiah Burchett, the 1st Earle of Hardwicke, James Naish, 1st Duke of Newcastle are contained in *Anson's Voyage* by Glyndur Williams.

Millechamps' Journal 1740-1744. National Maritime Museum.

van Keppel, Augustus: Journals, 1740-1744. Public Records Office.

A NOTE TO THE READER

It is said that writing is the purview of a vivid imagination and the observance of the human condition. While Leo Heaps had both of these qualities, the arc of his life is perhaps one of the more unusual trajectories of a human being — a man thrust into living and breathing the very subject matter of his books.

Whether it was his lifelong relationship with Hugh Hambleton, who later became a KGB operative for 30 years (*Hugh Hambleton, Spy: Thirty Years with the KGB*), or his sleuthing for rare artwork which produced the storied and adventurous *Log of the Centurion*, Leo Heaps was a sort of literary Walter Mitty; always searching for a life that transcended the norm. Whatever it was, Leo invariably found himself at the centre of it.

In 1942, after falling out of favour by the Canadian army, he joined the British First Airborne Division, where his one and only jump out of an airplane was into the war-ravaged fields of Ginkel Heath in Holland. After being caught in his underwear and put onto a train bound for a POW camp, he escaped and made his way back to England, where he was redeployed back to Holland to work with the Dutch resistance. These misadventures resulted in *The Grey Goose of Arnhem*, a gripping chronicle of the greatest mass escape of WW2.

After the war and a checkered career in real-estate, Leo settled on his real passions; the pursuit of fine art and writing. In 1972, a tip from an art dealer led him to the island of Guernsey, to buy a painting. Instead, he uncovered the long-hidden exquisite logs of Captain Philip Saumarez on board HMS Centurion, Lord Anson's flagship during his circumnavigation of 1740–44. *Log of The Centurion*, written by Leo Heaps, breathed new life into an ocean voyage which preceded Capt. Cook by almost twenty years.

Log of the Centurion was in its second printing when Leo Heaps's life was jarred into reality by a late-night phone call from Canada's national police force. His friend of almost forty years had been arrested and charged with being a Russian spy for almost three decades, compromising almost every member of NATO. While languishing in a British prison, Hugh Hambleton requested one visitor to tell his story; his only friend — Leo Heaps. *Hugh Hambleton, Spy: Thirty years with the KGB* revealed a mild-mannered professor turned double agent using code breaking equipment and a sophisticated spy network.

In 1978, during a trip to Canada's far north, Leo Heaps heard about a Russia spy satellite launched by the Soviet Union in 1977. A malfunction prevented safe separation of its onboard nuclear reactor when the satellite re-entered the Earth's atmosphere the following year prompting an extensive cleanup operation known as *Operation Morning Light*. The contents of the satellite, not to mention the radioactive debris became the subject of intense investigation and an environmental catastrophe for the local people. Through a series of circumstances, Leo Heaps managed to secure exclusive passage with the investigators into Cosmos 954, and reveal the true story.

As literary executor of the Leo Heaps estate, we are thrilled that audiences around the world can once again, enjoy these fine books. As historical works, their stories are timeless with each book an adventure in its own right.

Sapere Books is an exciting new publisher of brilliant fiction and popular history.

To find out more about our latest releases and our monthly bargain books visit our website:
saperebooks.com

Printed in Great Britain
by Amazon